What people are saying abou

Experience is the best teacher, and you're better off if you can learn from someone else's mistakes. Brian packs years worth of experience into one place: this book.

Michael Chanley

Director, International Network of Children's Ministry; Creator of cmconnect.org

Reading about somebody's past mistakes is like watching a train wreck in slow motion. At times I laughed, and at other times I felt extreme embarrassment for Brian's situation. However, there's something powerfully disarming in a book like this. In more than one chapter, I saw myself in exactly the same situation, and it's comforting to know that I wasn't alone in my failures. This is a must-read book for anyone in ministry! Don't reinvent the wheel—learn from Brian's pain!

Kenny Conley

NextGen Pastor, Gateway Church, Austin, Texas

Blog: childrensministryonline.com

Brian takes his years of experience and packages them in lessons that are painfully hilarious and insightful at the same time. If you have been a kids pastor for 2 days or 20 years, you'll benefit from the practical wisdom Brian learned the hard way. I hope you enjoy Brian's book as much as I did.

Sam Luce

Children's Pastor, Redeemer Church,

Utica, New York

Blog: samluce.com

As I read Brian's book, I was immediately drawn in by his candor and humor as he reveals some of the biggest mistakes he's made in ministry. I value his honesty in describing what most of us would rather fade into the shadows of the past. Not only did Brian grow from these mistakes, but also, he shares how we can avoid them. This is a great, encouraging resource for any kidmin leader.

Gina McClain
Children's Ministry Director
Faith Promise Church, Knoxville, Tennessee

Brian presents an authentic look into the heart of a children's pastor. His honesty and transparency allow other leaders to learn from his mistakes, and his wisdom provides practical ways for readers to avoid falling prey to the same leadership pitfalls. *I Blew It!* needs to be in the hands of every *new* children's minister and on the shelf of every *seasoned* children's ministry leader.

Scott Berkey
National Director
Children's Ministries Agency of Assemblies of God

Brian has done a great job of sharing his ministry experiences in a way that challenges every KidMin leader—not only to grow in ministry and leadership skills, but also to view every ministry experience from the Father's perspective. He gets it that ministry is not about abilities but about relationships—with God and with others.

Kathy Creasy
National Director of Children's Ministries
Church of God of Prophecy

Children's ministry can be a little overwhelming and scary at times. This book will help you put those fears to rest. The topics Brian addresses are some of the most practical I've ever seen. Use it to be inspired and educated—and to change lives!

Ryan Frank
Executive Director, KidzMatter, Inc.

Reading Brian Dollar's book was such an encouraging relief. I laughed out loud at his stories as I remembered many times *I blew it*, too. And I enjoyed reading the insights he has gained over the years as God has refined his youthful enthusiasm into seasoned wisdom. This book is a terrific resource for beginners in kidmin and should be a textbook for veterans who may think they "know it all." Brian has practical guidance for all of us who minister to children or lead those who do.

Karl Bastian a.k.a. "The Kidologist"
Founder of Kidology.org

It is so easy for young ministers to look at established kids' pastors like Brian and assume they never made any mistakes. In *I Blew It!*, Brian shares candidly about his failures. In the process, he provides encouragement to all of us that failure is not final. This book will both challenge and warm your heart.

Roger Fields
President of Kidz Blitz Ministries

Learning from your own mistakes is good, but learning from others is even better! Glance down through the chapter titles in Brian's book, and you may realize you've been making one of those statements recently. Warning, warning . . . flip to that chapter quickly and let Brian help steer you around the stress! *I Blew It!* is a great collection of practical, in-your-face guidance that will make you feel like you've got a personal mentor.

Tina Houser
Author
Publications Director, Kidzmatter, Inc.

I love this book! Brian speaks from experience with a relevant and engaging style. The mistakes he describes are common with children's ministry leaders, but they're avoidable—if you recognize them. I wish I'd had half this information when I started in children's ministry. It would have saved me from a lot of headaches! I highly recommend that every children's ministry leader *read this book*!

Greg Baird

Founder, KidMin360/KidMinJobs

I Blew It! is a candid, vulnerable look at the ministry mistakes that plague us all—pastors and volunteers alike. Brian Dollar is a recognized leader in children's ministry who is still in the trenches, leading children in our local church setting on a weekly basis. He is creative and talented, but most of all, he's a great storyteller! You'll laugh at Brian's crazy misadventures, and you'll be moved to tears by his deep heart issues. This book is essential for children's pastors and children's ministry leaders!

Rod Loy

Senior Pastor

First Assembly of God, North Little Rock, Arkansas

There are two significant ways of acquiring wisdom: mistakes and mentors. Brian Dollar shares with transparency how both of these have impacted his life and ministry. There is no doubt that ministry to children is of vital importance, and Brian shows how you can be effective in reaching children.

Dr. Alton Garrison

Assistant Superintendent Of the Assemblies of God

Brian Dollar is one of the greatest kids' pastors in the nation because he knows how to learn from his mistakes. As you will see in the pages of this book, he's learned a lot because he's messed up a lot . . . and now he passes those lessons on to us. *I Blew It!* is required reading for kids' pastors who want to make a huge difference in the next generation.

Scott Wilson

Senior Pastor

The Oaks Fellowship, Red Oak, Texas

I was Brian Dollar's pastor in his youth, and having four sons, I just "adopted" Brian as another "son." Brian allowed me to speak frankly with him, and I watched him develop in ministry and personal maturity. Brian is an exciting innovator who provides ministry resources for many ministries, and his newest book is a must-read for young ministers. Brian's honesty and insight are remarkable, and *I Blew It!* is a humorous "reality show" of how to overcome the pitfalls while maturing in ministry.

Tom Wilson, PhD

Pastor Emeritus

The Oaks Fellowship, Red Oak, Texas

Brian has been one of my closest friends for 20 years. He didn't just write about ideas—he has lived them. This book is an overflow of his personal relationship with Christ and a fruitful ministry. As I read it, I was engaged because of his blend of humor, scripture, and real life experiences. This isn't just for kids' pastors, it's valuable for the entire body of Christ.

John Van Pay

Lead Pastor

Gateway Fellowship; Helotes, Texas

Having known Brian for over 25 years, I am amazed at the man he has become. From our days as kids in Sunday school until now, he has consistently taken his mess and turned it into a success. I believe every church leader should read *I Blew It!* and apply the lessons Brian has learned.

Rusty Posey

Student Ministries Director

Northside Church, Texarkana, Texas

Brian Dollar brings a very seasoned and excellent approach to ministry to children and families. He combines fantastic creativity and "down-to-earth" practicality that keeps children engaged and changed. He is a role model for the next generation of children's ministry leaders. I highly recommend his new book, *I Blew It!*

Joey Ellis
AGWM Missionary to Children

Wow! Brian's candid honesty is a breath of fresh air. Whether you are just starting out in ministry or a seasoned veteran, there is much to be learned from Brian's experiences. I appreciate his transparency on issues that many leaders would prefer to sweep under a rug. While there is comedic relief in Brian's journey, there are rich lessons that will save you from having your own "I blew it" moment.

Joy Bowen
Coach and Specialist for Orange (WhatisOrange.org)
Blog: www.ImpulsiveJoy.com and
www.KidzPraise.com

This book is dedicated to . . .

Rev. Brent Williams

Thanks for taking a punk kid and believing God could transform him into something worthy of His calling. I love you and am thankful for your influence in my life.

Rev. Scott Wilson

Who knows why you saw what you did in me at such a young age? I will forever be grateful for the opportunities you gave me and the lessons you taught me. Thank you for pushing me to be passionate in all things.

Dr. Tom Wilson

You have always been like a spiritual father to me. Thank you for showing me how to value God's Word and prayer. You are the epitome of a pastor's heart.

Pastor Rod Loy

Words cannot express what you mean to me as a mentor, pastor, and friend. Thank you for the repeated risks you have taken to ensure my success—personally and spiritually. I'm humbled to serve you. I hope to always make you proud.

Contents

Acknowledgements

I want to thank my amazing High Voltage Kids Ministry team of volunteers and staff. You demonstrate the heart of Christ every week to over 600 children. This book is a testimony to the commitment each of you has to building His kingdom.

Special thanks to the leadership and congregation of First Assembly of God in North Little Rock, Arkansas. You give me more opportunities to make a difference than any other Kids Pastor I know. Thanks for allowing me to take what I have learned and share it with others.

Thanks to these Kids Ministry heroes who have shaped my ministry, both from up close and far away: Jim Wideman, Craig Jutila, Reggie Joiner, Larry Fowler, and Sue Miller.

Thanks to Pastor Steve Flores for being a steadfast friend and Christlike model for me. You helped me through one of the most difficult seasons of my life.

Thanks to my new friend, Pat Springle. You pushed me to make this book less about strategies and more about heart. You kept me on track and on point. Thanks for making my words come to life in a big, heartfelt way.

Thanks to my grandfather, Rev. L.W. Dollar. You have always been my hero! Thank you for demonstrating a lifetime of faithfulness to God!

Special thanks to my parents, Roger and Elaine, and my sister, Karen. You have always believed in me and prayed for me. Thanks for your unconditional love and grace!

Thanks to my two children, Ashton and Jordan. You make my life bright with your love and energy. I love you and am so proud of how you both continue to pursue Jesus with all your heart. I can't wait to see all He does through you!

An extra special thanks to my wife, Cherith. You are the love of my life. You have been more patient, forgiving, and gracious than anyone will ever know. Thank you for sticking by me in my darkest hours and showing me what a true woman of God looks like. I love you.

Foreword

All of us have made mistakes. In fact, we've failed time and time again. We don't like to talk about them. We'd much rather talk about our successes, but without failures, there would be no successes. If we respond in faith, mistakes become the stepping-stones of growth. I'm excited about Brian's book and the honor he gave me to write the foreword. Finally, someone is willing to be honest about the many failures on the road to success. Parents aren't perfect. Kids aren't perfect either. That's hard for some parents to admit. And certainly, kids' pastors and leaders blow it and suffer the consequences. We don't have a "Get Out of Jail Free" card to use whenever we need it. No one does! Although we all blow it on a regular basis, few of us are skilled at handling failure. That's why Brian's book about his mistakes excites me.

One of my favorite Michael Jordan commercials reminds us that failure doesn't have to stop us or slow us down. We all think of MJ as one of the most successful athletes of all time, but he was a champion of failure. Jordan admits, "I've missed more than 9000 shots in my career. I've lost almost 300 games. 26 times, I've been trusted to take the game winning shot and missed. I've failed over and over and over again in my life. And that is why I succeed." Michael Jordan knows that it's not the mistake that stops us, but how we respond to the mistake that counts! When we fail, we have the ultimate resource. King Solomon said, "A righteous man may have many troubles, but the LORD delivers him from them all" (Psalms 34:19).

I'm a good ole boy from Alabama, and to be honest, I'm a lot like Forrest Gump. When I was growing up, my Mom told me a lot of very useful advice. She said that experience is the best teacher, but the classroom doesn't have to be your own failures. If we'll pay attention, Brian will be one of our best teachers, and we'll learn how to avoid making the mistakes he made—or if we've already made them, we can at least learn from him how to handle them with courage and faith. These lessons are priceless. That's true wisdom. Mom also told me, "Don't make the same mistake twice." She said, "There are plenty of others for you to make." If only I'd listened to Mom! And now, if only we'll listen to Brian.

As a children's pastor or volunteer leader, you have the privilege of setting an example for those you lead. Paul wrote to Timothy, his young protégé, "Don't let anyone look down on you because you are young, but set an example for the believers in speech, in conduct, in love, in faith and in purity" (1 Timothy 4:12). My prayer for you is that you learn important lessons from these pages and pass them down to those you lead so the Kingdom of God will be strengthened and expanded. That's my prayer for you. And that's my prayer for me!

Jim Wideman
Jim Wideman Ministries
Murfreesboro, Tennessee

Introduction:
Learning the Hard Way

I hate to make mistakes. I hate it even more when people notice when I've messed up—and they usually do. But I really hate it when I don't learn from my mistakes. Then they're wasted. All of us have blunders and goofs from time to time, but some of mine have been utterly idiotic. Let me tell you about one of them.

Not long after I'd become the Kids Pastor at our church, I was preparing for one of the most important events of the year: our annual Easter egg hunt. I'd done most of the planning by myself, and I was sure it was going to be terrific. I was so confident in my plans that I had fantasies about all the praise and thanks I'd receive from the incredible event. It was going to be the most magnificent, most memorable Easter egg hunt anyone would ever remember. On Palm Sunday, the week before, I announced to the congregation in our worship services: "You don't want to miss the Easter egg hunt next Saturday morning. It'll be unbelievable and unforgettable!" And it was.

Our church doesn't have very many large grassy areas, so I had to be very selective about where I put the different age groups for the egg hunt. I chose a long, narrow grassy area for the elementary kids, but I was a little puzzled where to put the preschool kids. Then, I found it—the perfect place for our preschool egg hunt. It was a steep bank with big rocks, and it plunged down into a drainage ditch. Early that morning, I gave directions to our team to hide the plastic eggs under and around all the rocks on the bank. I thought, *What perfect hiding spots! These kids will have a ball!*

The time came for the preschool egg hunt. The children lined up at the edge of the ditch. They were ready to go! I blew the whistle, and the hunt began. In a matter of seconds, little kids were falling down the hill into the rocks. Their knees were bleeding, and their eyes were full of tears, but they were determined to find the colored plastic eggs. When they opened them, they got a big surprise. At a discount store, I'd bought Atomic Fireballs, jawbreakers, and all kinds of other candies that could be lethal choking hazards for preschoolers.

The realization of how bad I had messed up came slowly. A little blood . . . no big deal. A few tears . . . completely expected. But then my pastor's wife walked over and held up an Atomic Fireball. She stared at me with a puzzled look, shook her head, and said, "Really, Brian? Atomic Fireballs? Really?"

At that moment, I knew I was in big trouble. Then reality hit me like a two-ton truck: Parents were furious with me. Some glared at me in disbelief, but others were so angry they avoided eye contact. My volunteers couldn't believe I was so stupid, and my pastor was more than disappointed at my lack of wisdom.

At that moment, I had to make a choice. Do I make excuses? Will I defend my decisions and plans? Can I blame someone else? Should I shrug my shoulders and act like nothing's wrong? Do I ignore it for a few days and hope the anger blows over? Or will I find the courage to own my mistakes and learn from them?

All of us face these questions when we make mistakes—and we certainly are going to make plenty of them. We're human, and mistakes are a normal part of life. Ministry (and every other part of life) is packed with difficult choices that require wisdom, and often, we have to face problems we've never encountered before. Mistakes are inevitable—sometimes really big ones! No matter how hard we try to do things right, the question isn't "Will I make mistakes?" but "How will I respond to my mistakes?"

A long time ago, I made a commitment to avoid wasting my mistakes because they are some of the best learning opportunities in life. Whenever I mess up, I try to ask four important questions:

—Why did it happen? Was it a lack of planning, unrealistic expectations, poor communication, wrong motives, unforeseen obstacles, or some other reason?

—Was it avoidable? Many of our goofs can be avoided with better planning, communication, and execution, but some can't.

—If it could have been avoided, what specifically could I have done to prevent it?

—What do I need to know, be, or do to avoid repeating the mistake?

People gain wisdom in three different ways. Some people go straight to the Bible and make changes based on the eternal wisdom of the Scriptures. More people observe others' mistakes—and the painful consequences—and learn the lessons before having to make the mistakes themselves. But most of us learn only in the hard school of experience. This book is a collection of stories (some funny, some devastating), documenting mistakes I've made and the lessons I've learned in more than twenty years of kids' ministry. I hope you

> This book is a collection of stories (some funny, some devastating), documenting mistakes I've made and the lessons I've learned in more than twenty years of kids' ministry. I hope you can learn from my mistakes so you don't have to make them yourself.

can learn from my mistakes so you don't have to make them yourself.

Terrific People, a Tough Job

Children's ministers are some of the most wonderful people I know. They're passionate about reaching kids for Christ and helping parents love their sons and daughters. They're compassionate, sensitive people, and they know how to have fun. I love hanging out with them! Like most people, they carry some deep hurts from painful past experiences. Their ministry to kids helps to fill their emotional tanks, but too often, these tanks are drained when they don't feel respected by other leaders in the church because their ministry is "only working with children."

In many churches, people who minister to children are taken for granted. The pastor and other leaders plan a big outreach, discipleship program, or concert, and the first question asked is, "What will we do with the children?" The assumption is that the workers in the children's ministry are always available to step up to handle every need. And they are, but at a huge sacrifice. Most people in the church—including the pastor and the staff—seldom realize that many who work in the children's ministry don't get to come to church-wide events because they serve sacrificially to care for people's kids.

Years ago, they used to go to the Sunday night or Wednesday night services, but in recent years, many churches have done away with those times of corporate worship. Now, there's nothing the kids' ministry staff and volunteers can attend. Missing once or twice (or a dozen times) may not matter much, but after many months, they crave the opportunity to be fed from the Word and worship with other adults. I've talked to some kids' ministry workers who haven't been in their church's regular worship service in years. It hurts—and it's confusing—to be taken for granted. When this happens, the joy of serving Christ and pouring life into kids gradually erodes and is replaced with a nagging resentment. The good news is that it doesn't have to be this way.

Three Types of Roles

In churches throughout the country, ministries to children are considered absolutely essential. The size and resources of the church, however, determine who is in charge of this work.

Some churches have full-time kids' ministry pastors. They understand the complexity of recruiting, training, and working with volunteers, finding life-changing curriculum, and involving parents. These kids' pastors are dedicated and determined. They attend conferences and read articles, books, and blogs to enhance their skills, but they often struggle to be respected by other members of the pastoral staff.

Many churches have part-time kids' ministry pastors who work about 5–10 hours each week in the office, but in fact, they're expected to do almost as much work as a full-time kids' ministry pastor. They'd love to have the time to read and go to conferences to enhance their skills, but they simply don't have time for much of that. They often have a full-time job outside the church, and they spend all their time simply trying to hold things together.

Countless smaller churches have volunteer kids' ministry pastors or directors who depend on their pastor to point them to resources. They struggle to find enough people to fill slots in each age group, and they often have to fill in for those who can't make it that week. They work like crazy and often feel unappreciated.

My Hope for You

Leaders in all three groups can learn from my mistakes. (I'm not sure if that's good for my reputation, but it's true.) The stories and principles in this book are designed to assure you that making mistakes is normal, but if we have the courage to ask hard questions, we can learn important lessons from our failures. It's easy to excuse our flaws, blame others, or try to ignore the consequences of our mistakes, but those choices only lead to more head-aches and heartaches. If we make honest evaluation part of our daily lives, we can live more fully in God's grace and truth.

> I hope my experiences encourage you to be honest about your own mistakes, but even more, I hope they inspire you to cling to God more tightly than ever.

In this book, I've identified and described twelve mistakes I've made in my life and ministry. I'm not implying that every person reading this book has made or is making all of these, but these are the ones that surface most often in my conversations with people who minister to children. If you aren't wrestling with one or two of them now, just wait—you probably will in the near future.

I hope my experiences encourage you to be honest about your own mistakes, but even more, I hope they inspire you to cling to God more tightly than ever. The demands of working with children, church staff, volunteers, and parents can feel overwhelming. We will eventually burn out if we let ministry take God's rightful place in our hearts. Everything we are and everything we do must be—and can be—an overflow of our love for God as we respond to His amazing love for us.

In the Gospel of John, we find Jesus and the disciples at an important feast in Jerusalem. On the last day, the most important day of the celebration, Jesus stood up and cried out, "Let anyone who is thirsty come to me and drink. Whoever believes in me, as Scripture has said, rivers of living water will flow from within them." To make sure his readers (including you and I) understand, John explained, "By this he meant the Spirit, whom those who believed in him were later to receive" (John 7:37-39).

In my interactions with people involved in children's ministries around the country, I've noticed they're very thirsty—not just for ministry strategies and tools, but even more, to know and love Jesus more deeply. I hope God uses this book to help quench your thirst for Him.

"I know where I'm going and how to get there."

1

When I was in college, I wanted to get involved in reaching students with the gospel. I didn't want to wait until I graduated to figure out what God wanted me to do with my life. At a summer camp, I met Scott Wilson, a powerful preacher and youth pastor. Scott is a passionate, driven, anointed leader. I liked him, and I respected his heart for the Lord. I wanted to spend time with him and soak up everything he could teach me.

I began working with Scott in the Youth Ministry Intern Program at Oak Cliff Assembly of God (now called The Oaks Fellowship) in Dallas. Eventually, Scott asked me to lead the interns who were attending a local Bible college. It was my role to teach them the practical side of ministry. I loved it, and it was terrific training for me as I prepared to become a youth pastor after I graduated. Of course, all this was designed to equip me to be a senior pastor one day. I had no question this was God's plan for my life.

One day our Senior Pastor, Tom Wilson, approached me. He said, "Brian, our Children's Pastor is leaving. Would you be willing to step in and lead the kids' ministry for a few weeks while we look for the right person for this role?"

Instantly, I replied, "Sure! I'd be happy to. When do I start?"

Without a second of hesitation, he answered, "This week."

No problem. I like a challenge, and I like kids. Kids are fun, and I relate to them pretty easily. Actually, I had no idea what I was doing in leading a children's ministry, but I was willing to give it my best shot.

The first few weeks were exhilarating. I loved it! And for some strange reason, we actually grew during the first few months I was in my new role. I think we grew because I prayed daily and desperately, "God, what am I supposed to do with these kids? I don't have a clue." The Lord seemed to delight in my prayers, and He blessed us.

After about six months, it dawned on me that I hadn't noticed many applicants for the Children's Pastor position coming by for interviews. In fact, there weren't any at all. One day, I asked Pastor Wilson, "Um, I haven't seen any of the candidates you mentioned who might be coming to interview to be our Children's Pastor. What's the status on all that?"

He didn't hesitate a second. He told me, "Brian, you're doing a great job, and we're growing. Let's just keep doing what we're doing for a little while longer."

Of course, many years later, I understood what he really meant: "Why would we want to *pay* someone when you're willing to do it for *free*?" I was having a great time, so I didn't mind.

After about three years in this role as a volunteer Children's Pastor—you read that correctly, three years—I was ready to graduate from college. It was time to get serious about my future as a youth pastor. I made an appointment with Pastor Wilson, and I prepared my speech. I planned to say, "Pastor Wilson, thank you for letting me be the Children's Pastor for these years. It's been great, but I have other plans. If you don't have a youth ministry position for me here at the church, then I'm going to have to start circulating my resume. After all, I'm supposed to be a youth pastor for a couple years and then become a senior pastor. That's the plan."

I was ready for the meeting, but I thought it would be a good idea to take a few minutes to pray. Just before the time I was to meet with Pastor Wilson, I found an empty Sunday school room on the third floor of the church and began to tell God what He needed to do for me. I prayed, "God, You're going to have to help him understand my plan. Help him not get upset when I tell him what I want to do."

> The Lord said, "Really? I'm glad you have this wonderful plan, Brian. Have you ever thought to ask Me what *My* plan is for you?"

Now, I don't use the phrase "God spoke to me" very often, but at that moment, I felt as though an almost audible voice spoke to me. Actually, it confronted me. The Lord said, "Really? I'm glad you have this wonderful plan, Brian. Have you ever thought to ask Me what *My* plan is for you?"

Yikes! Talk about a "shame grenade"! God blew me up. I had assumed that all I needed was for God to pave the way for my plans. It had never occurred to me that He might have different plans. I felt like the dumbest person on the planet, but I also realized God had done something very special for me. He hadn't allowed me to continue on my self-absorbed journey. He had broken through to get my attention and redirect me. It was a wonderful moment of grace.

As I sat on the floor of that Sunday school room, reflecting on what God had said to me, He reminded me what Jesus told His followers on the night before He died. In a garden outside Jerusalem, He explained, "I am the vine; you are the branches. If a man remains in me and I in him, he will bear much fruit; apart from me you can do nothing" (John 15:5). The Lord said, "Brian, you need to remember that I am the vine and you are the branch. Without Me, you can do nothing. Let's not go with *your* plan. Let's go with *My* plan."

But God wasn't finished. As clearly as anything ever communicated to me, He said, "I want you to remain in children's ministry."

It was a dramatic, unexpected moment, and it definitely changed my direction. A few minutes later, I walked in to Pastor Wilson's office and told him that God had spoken to my heart that He wanted me to remain as the Children's Pastor. He smiled and said, "Brian, I was just praying before you walked in here: 'Lord, let him have the desire for children's ministry because we just don't have a position available in youth ministry right now.' If you had insisted on youth ministry, I would have had to let you go."

I had lived for three years with the clear, strong—but wrong—assumption that God was thrilled to bless my plans for my future. In only a few minutes, God had turned all this upside down and inside out. I realized I'd made a serious miscalculation about God's direction for my life. The image that perfectly captures my thoughts at that time is a man trying to hack his way through an impenetrable jungle with a dull machete, and he's forgotten that his father owns a bulldozer! He can keep hacking away and making little progress, or he can call his dad for help. During all that time, I had failed to call on my Father for help. When He finally took the initiative to call me, I thought it was a good idea to answer!

**My mistake: Accepting God's destination,
but forging my own path to get there.**

Assumptions and Conclusions

Pastor and author, Tim Keller, advises us, "Don't confuse your *agenda for* God with *faith in* God."[1] Too often, we go to God with our plans, our desires, and in fact, our demands that He should jump through our hoops. Oh, we would never put it that way, but when God doesn't do what we expect Him to do for us, we whine and feel that He's let us down. Genuine faith goes to Him with a thankful heart and open hands—ready to accept whatever He puts in them. How often do we allow our assumptions and presuppositions to cloud our understanding of God's will? We think we know exactly where our lives should go, and we ask God's blessing to help us get there smoothly and easily. We may not have even asked Him to show us His will, and if He had, we might have argued with Him! We draw wrong conclusions about the destination, and we often have misperceptions about the path He wants us to walk.

We can make this mistake in any area of life: marriage, parenting, work, friendships, finances, and ministry (to name a few). We may have been dating someone for years and have assumed he or she is the right person to marry, but we haven't asked God for direction. We may have held a job for a long time with the assumption that we should work for that company in that role, and we haven't been open to God's whispers to redirect us. We may have lived under our parents' expectations for us to go to a certain school or work in a particular career, and we haven't asked God to guide us.

Sometimes, we don't even think about praying. We may be so sure we know the right way that we don't feel any need for God's power and direction, or we may be so busy that we forget to pray. But there might be a deeper issue: Secretly, we may not want God to show us His path. We have it all planned out in our minds, and we aren't going to let anybody—even God—get in our way. We're sure we know who we should marry, how to raise our kids, what kind of job we should have, how to spend our money, and where to serve God in ministry, so we don't even ask. For a long time, we can rock along without a thought that we need to go deeper with God, but sooner or later, He gets our attention. That's what happened to me before I met with Pastor Wilson that day.

During the summer camp years earlier when I met Scott Wilson, I spent hours praying for God's wisdom about becoming a full-time minister. God showed me clearly that He wanted me to serve as a full-time minister at some point in the future, but I made the colossal (and wrong) assumption that I knew exactly what specific role He wanted me to play. I hadn't even thought to ask Him if He wanted me to be a youth pastor and then a senior pastor. I was *absolutely sure* that was His plan. Until God spoke to me in the Sunday school room before my meeting with Pastor Wilson, I hadn't spent a single minute asking Him for direction. Dumb. Really dumb.

It's like your boss telling you, "The company just bought a new office building, and I have a brand new office for you. Meet me there in the morning at 8:00." He knows where the office is located. He's been there, and he knows the streets. But you don't ask for directions, and you don't even ask for the address. You know the destination, but you don't have a clue about the path to get there. That's the epitome of foolishness. Sadly, some of us have a habit of making this mistake. We pray to God for vision for our lives, our families, and our ministries. He gives us a picture of the future, and we start charging after that vision wholeheartedly without stopping to ask Him for specific directions.

We aren't alone in making this mistake. God gave Abraham a glowing promise: "I will make you into a great nation and I will bless you" (Genesis 12:2). Abraham accepted God's promise, but when his expectations weren't fulfilled in his time frame, Abraham carved out his own plans to have children. He slept with his wife's servant, Hagar, in an attempt to get him to the destination in a hurry. By this time, Abraham and Sarah were old—far past the age to have children. He assumed that if God's plan was for him to be the father of many nations, then he'd better start trying to make it happen! He accepted God's destination, but tried to forge his own path. The result was family strife, bitterness, and centuries of conflict in the Middle East—quite a legacy.

Abraham's example of impatience and wrong assumptions isn't an isolated case. I've done it, and you've probably done it, too. We believe God has called us to fulfill a certain role or achieve a particular goal, but we make the assumption that we know how it's going to happen. These assumptions may be prompted by ignorance or pride. Whatever the cause, they lead us into big trouble. Subtly and gradually, we assume that God has to play by our rules. When times get tough and our hopes are delayed or shattered, we get mad. We're either angry with God for letting us down, or we're mad at ourselves for being such a loser. Neither of these conclusions leads us to wisdom, joy, and strength.

Tender and Open

In the Bible, we find some wonderful examples of tender hearts and open minds. Joseph is one of the best. In two dreams when he was a young man, God revealed to Joseph that he would one day become ruler over his brothers and parents. However, Joseph could never have imagined God's script for his life's story. When he told his family about his dreams, he had no idea he would be betrayed by his brothers, sold into slavery in Egypt, accused of a crime he didn't commit, rot away for years in prison, interpret the pharaoh's dreams about fat and skinny cows, become prime minister of the most powerful nation on earth, and save his family (and Egypt) from a devastating famine.

At any point in this incredible journey, he could have wallowed in self-pity, hated his brothers, blamed God, and given up on everything—but he didn't. Through it all, he trusted God to lead him . . . in God's way and in God's timing. When the time was right and opportunity knocked, Joseph was ready. During the long years of disappointment, he kept trusting God and believing that God would lead him—even in the darkest times of his life.

Our tendency is to ask God to show us His ultimate destination for our lives and then try to figure out the path on our own. When He gives us a glimpse of His vision for our future, we start sketching a plan in our own minds. We don't pray, "Lord, what's the next step?" If we were to think for a second, we'd realize the important truth: The God who revealed the destination will also reveal the path!

When we try to get God to fulfill our plans, we reverse roles with him: He becomes our servant, and we try to be the boss. Psychologist Larry Crabb says that many of us treat God like "a specially attentive waiter."[2] When we get good service from Him, we give Him a tip of praise. But when we don't get what we want when we want it, we complain about His poor service. This is the mistake Adam and Eve made in the Garden, and it's one we often make today. We insist on running our own lives, accomplishing our own goals, and using God instead of loving and serving Him. We think we know better than God how our lives should work out.

What does this assumption look like? There are countless forms, but here are a few examples:

—We believe, "God doesn't want me to be poor," so we look for a job so we can make the most money without a thought about where God might want us to work.

—We're sure, "God wants me to be happy," so we entertain ourselves to numb the pain of an empty life instead of digging deep to discover God's higher purpose for our lives.

—We assume, "I need a master's degree to be a teacher in the kids' ministry so I can do a good job teaching God's Word."

—Single people may believe, "I don't have any kids of my own, so I don't know how to minister to children. I'm disqualified."

—We think, "God certainly doesn't want me to feel lonely," so we jump in bed before we're married.

—We're certain that applause is a sign of God's blessing, so we live to make people laugh to win approval.

—We may conclude, "If I sacrifice my time to minister to kids, I'll always feel great and be treated like a hero. That's what I live for."

—Like the disciples, we have a hard time believing that suffering is central to God's plan, so we try to avoid it at all costs.

Discovering God's path isn't like sitting in the tower at the airport with air traffic controllers and watching every movement of every plane in the sky. God seldom gives us more information than the next step. His wisdom is like a flashlight on a dark night. We can see just far enough ahead to keep us on the path, but not much farther. But it's enough, and it's all we really need. Staying on the path, though, requires one essential character quality: trust.

Real Faith

The reason we try to forge our own path is because we really don't trust God to lead us. You're probably thinking, "Brian, how can you even suggest that I don't trust God? I've accepted Christ as my Savior. I've accepted God's call on my life to care for kids. Of course I trust Him."

Really? Then why do you get upset when things don't go the way you planned? Isn't it because God didn't follow your script?

Solomon wrote, "Trust in the LORD with all your heart and lean not on your own understanding; in all your ways acknowledge him, and he will make your paths straight" (Proverbs 3:5-6). We get excited when we read this verse. We love the promise of straight paths. God promises to make our paths straight so that we can accomplish His objectives. We want this, don't we? Interestingly, the Hebrew word in this verse translated "straight" means more than just guidance. It literally means God removes obstacles, making a smooth path or way of life to bring us to the appointed goal. It's not about guidance to an ultimate end, but instead, it's the power to continue moving forward on the right path one step at a time. That's an awesome promise!

When we think of a straight path, we may think it means the most direct line between two points. That's basic geometry. We assume, "Obviously, if God wants me to arrive at the ultimate destination He has revealed to me, I need to take the quickest, smoothest, obstacle-free path. I'll look for the shortest and easiest path—that's the one I'm supposed to take."

The path, though, isn't primarily about how to get from Point A to Point B. In fact, I think we miss the whole point of the passage when we read it as a promise of a trouble-free life. If we look more closely, we'll see some important conditions to the promise. Solomon instructed us to trust God with "all" our hearts and acknowledge Him in "all" our ways. The passage, then, is more about the purity of our devotion than the promise of a destination. We see this pattern throughout the Scriptures. The "straight path" for Abraham, Joseph, Paul, Peter, and the people listed in Hebrews 11 certainly wasn't smooth and easy! And if we want to look at the supreme example of someone who was completely devoted to the Father, we can look at Jesus. His path led Him to the mountain of transfiguration and the valley of rejection and torture. But through it all, He stayed firmly on the path the Father laid out for Him. That's our task, too.

The Message translates the passage in Proverbs: "Listen for God's voice in everything you do, everywhere you go." For three years when I'd assumed I was going to be a youth pastor and then a senior pastor, I hadn't listened to God's voice. Finally, in the Sunday school room before I met with Pastor Wilson, God broke through so loudly that I had to listen!

The requirement of "all" asks for more than some of us want to give. Trusting God with our whole heart means we hold nothing back. We give Him the keys to every room in our hearts, and we acknowledge that He has the perfect right to direct our lives—into glorious light and into painful darkness. He is no longer our waiter; we are now His.

Rod Loy, my pastor, friend, and mentor, says that many people in the American church have rewritten Proverbs 3:5,6:

> I'll trust in the Lord as much as I'm able—as long as it doesn't cost me too much, make life inconvenient, or keep me from fitting in with everyone around me. I expect Him to bless my plans. I acknowledge Him as my Lord, but I don't really let Him affect the details of my life. I do what I want, when I want, and how I want. I won't allow anyone, including God, to impose what I think are unrealistic expectations on me. Then, because I've given Him some trust and followed Him with part of my life, He better make my paths straight.

What does it mean to trust God with all your heart? What does it mean to acknowledge Him in all your ways? I'm afraid most of us have no clue what it really means.

What does it mean to trust God with all your heart? What does it mean to acknowledge Him in all your ways? I'm afraid most of us have no clue what it really means. It's not something you see much in today's society—or even in today's churches. We live in an incredibly self-absorbed world. We enjoy all kinds of modern conveniences and technology, but we've let drive-thru windows, ATMs, and online shopping convince us that spiritual life should be just as effortless. And since all of these things make a king out of the consumer, we think we're the center of the universe! People have always been self-absorbed, but never in history has society reinforced this assumption so powerfully. Our "on demand" culture causes us to adopt a mindset that's the opposite of being totally dependent on God. We're busy, we're important, and we know what makes us happy. In fact, we *deserve* to be happy and comfortable! Oh, we don't want to leave God out, but we sure don't want Him to interfere with our plans. We've made a halfway commitment acceptable. Sadly, a some-of-the-time, part-of-the-way commitment is the norm for many Christians—even those involved in ministry.

To trust God with all our heart, we trust God more than our own ability to come up with a reasonable plan. Solomon told us, "Lean not on your own understanding." We don't do that very well, do we? More often, we think, *I have so many great plans, God. I'm sure you want to bless them!*

We plot, plan, strategize, and scheme to make our paths straight. But self-absorption only makes our path more crooked, dark, and confusing. Trusting God with all your heart begins with a radical but foundational belief that His plan is better than your plan.

—His plan for relationships is better than your plan.

—His plan for your calling is better than your plan.

—His plan for family is better than your plan.

—His plan for your finances is better than your plan.

—His plan for your future is better than your plan.

In every area of your life, His plan beats your plan. His plan, no matter how crooked and convoluted it may seem at the moment, is perfectly straight in God's eyes. Your plan may sound good late at night when you're daydreaming about being good-looking, rich, and popular, but it soon becomes crooked and confusing because it misses the most important element on the journey: loving God with all our heart and letting His love overflow in every relationship, plan, and activity.

God's path is often very different from what we expected. We call the Christian life "an adventure," and adventures always involve unexpected dangers and unforeseen detours. Some of us thrive on risk, but others feel very uncomfortable with anything that seems out of our control. God doesn't ask us to face the unknown alone. He has promised to lead us, to be with us, and to bless us as we walk on smooth paths as well as rocky ones. Even when we feel lost, He's right there beside us. We don't trust in our ability to figure things out; we trust in Him.

If you can't accept the simple fact that God's plan is based on His infinite wisdom, goodness, and strength, you'll never be able to trust Him with all your heart. Learning to trust Him like this often is a very hard lesson to learn. It's been tough for me. Too often, I don't turn to Him until all my plans (including my back-up ones) have failed miserably. Finally, I remember that I should have asked God for wisdom instead of assuming he'd bless my plans. Sometimes, I've prayed, "God, I've messed this up so badly, trusting myself, that I now realize my only hope is to trust You to get me out of this trouble." It's kind of like Peter realizing he was sinking when he stepped out of the boat to walk on the water: "Jesus, save me!" Thank God, He responds to that kind of prayer. He reminds us of His presence, assures us of His love and power, and graciously puts us back on the straight path. Some of us, though, are slow learners. As soon as things are going better, we go back to trusting our plan instead of God's. When we forget to trust in God's goodness, greatness, and wisdom, our lives look like a schizophrenic hiker—on the path for a little while, off the path and backtracking, back on the path, off the path . . .

Life goes a lot better when we learn to go to God first instead of as a last resort.

The only way to stay on the straight path is to trust God with all your heart and acknowledge Him in all your ways. Life goes a lot better when we learn to go to God first instead of as a last resort. Some people might ask, "Brian, are you saying if I do this that I won't have any problems? That my life will be worry free?"

Certainly not. Jesus said, "In this world you will have trouble" (John 16:33). Pastor Rod describes realistic expectations:

> Real faith is like having spiritual shock absorbers. When you trust in God with all your heart and acknowledge Him in all your ways, He'll give you the strength to stay on the straight path and roll over the bumps and obstacles of life. On your own, they would bounce you around and throw you off track. You'd be back on a confusing, bumpy, circling path to nowhere. But when you're fully committed to God, He gives you grace to handle the inevitable bumps in the road so you can stay on the straight path.

You're reading this book because you want your life to count. You care deeply about kids, and you want to see them respond to the incredible love of

Christ. The first priority for all of us is to stay connected to the vine. Busyness is a poor substitute for real faith, and the enthusiasm we felt for kids' ministry in the beginning will eventually fade and leave us stale, empty, and angry. The only way we'll thrive as Christians and as kids' ministers is for us to trust God with our whole hearts, listen carefully to Him, cling to Him in good times and bad, and let His love, power, and wisdom overflow from full hearts.

When I left Pastor Wilson's office after telling him that God wanted me to remain as the children's pastor, I felt a deep sense of relief that the decision was God's instead of mine. I was thankful for God's grace in stepping in to redirect me even when I hadn't asked Him for guidance. And my mind raced with ideas about how God might use our ministry to shape the lives of kids in our community. Like never before, I experienced an amazing blend of peace, clarity, enthusiasm, and trust in God. It was a turning point in my life.

When we first get involved in ministry, it's usually because someone says, "Hey, we could use some help. Will you come to work with us for a few weeks?" There's no dramatic calling and no moment of *Shekinah* glory. But after a while, we need to ask God if we're in the right place so that our talents and gifts, our desires, and His calling all fit together. Without clear direction from God and a sense of His presence all along the way, we eventually burn out or drop out.

The first mistake we can make is to forget God while we're busy serving Him. Don't do that. In fact, don't let anything push Jesus out of the center of your affections. King David had a lot of pressure on him, and he made plenty of mistakes. But in many of his psalms, he recognized the ultimate importance of putting his relationship with God first. He wrote, "Delight yourself in the Lord and he will give you the desires of your heart" (Psalm 37:4). I don't think this is a formula to get whatever we want. In fact, I think it means that when we delight in God's love, presence, and power, He radically changes our desires. Gradually, we love what He loves, are hurt by what hurts Him, and care about the things that are most on His heart. It won't happen by magic, but only by tenaciously staying on God's path and walking arm in arm with Him.

To stay on God's path, ask, listen, and obey.

Think about it...

1. What are some problems that can happen when we assume we know God's plan without even asking Him to show us?

2. Why do some of us treat God like a "specially attentive waiter"?

3. When was a time when you genuinely delighted in God? What was going on? How did it affect your relationship with God, your relationships with others, and your motivation to serve Him?

4. Take a few minutes now to let God speak to your heart about the importance of delighting in Him. If He shows you that you've been trusting in yourself or gotten too busy, thank Him for His forgiveness, and enjoy His love.

"This is gonna be great!" 2

When I accepted the full-time position as Kids Pastor at Oak Cliff Assembly of God, I quickly got to work. I prayed a lot during those early days because I had no idea what I was doing. I was a young, single man, fresh out of college. Of course, I had no children of my own, but Pastor Wilson gave me the assignment of leading children in their spiritual journey. I was excited, but I felt like a fish out of water. I had some ideas about some programs we could launch, but I didn't have a lot of confidence in my planning abilities. I asked God for wisdom, and the Lord came through. We had several successful outreaches and events during my first year. God gave me some novel ideas on how to raise funds for our ministry. (We had a very limited budget. Ever been there?). I prayed and God answered.

Gradually, I began to realize that God had gifted me with creativity. I was very thankful for that. It takes real creativity to capture the attention of an ADHD first grader and keep it long enough for him to learn something that could change his life forever. I wanted to come up with programs that would make the Bible come alive for our kids. Creativity can be either a blessing or a curse. I quickly discovered that not all of my "amazing ideas" turn out the way I plan.

In a summer, not long after I took the role as the full-time Kids Pastor, we held Vacation Bible School. For the curriculum, we focused on the life of

Moses. We taught the kids that Moses floated in a basket as a baby and was adopted by the pharaoh's daughter. We learned about Moses running from Egypt and becoming a shepherd in the wilderness. There, God appeared to him in a burning bush and called him to lead the children of Israel out of slavery. Children love stories, and I was confident that this one would capture their hearts. All of this was good, but it seemed to lack some excitement. I wanted to create something really special to make the story of the exodus come alive for them. As I prepared the lessons, I tried to come up with just the right thing to help them understand God's power in freeing His people from Egypt.

That's when it hit me! It was an idea so clever that I almost gave myself a pat on the back. I told myself, "This is going to be awesome!" We were going to take the kids on The Plagues Tour.

A few months before, I had visited a local outreach event called "Hell House." In this event, groups of people are taken on a guided tour through many scenes depicting sinful, destructive behaviors: drug use, suicide, murder, abortion, hatred, and other kinds of sins. It was powerful and effective. The lives of many teenagers and adults had been changed as a result of this dynamic, interactive outreach.

As I prepared for Vacation Bible School, I wondered, *What if I do my own version of Hell House? What if I take this idea and apply it to Moses and the Exodus? This will be great!*

The Plagues Tour was designed to give kids a real-life experience of what it was like for the Egyptians to go through each of the ten plagues. They were so painful and destructive that the pharaoh finally released the slaves and asked them to leave the country. To make this work, we planned to divide the kids up in groups of ten (one for each plague), have one of our leaders be the tour guide, then lead them down our Kids Ministry hallway from room to room. If it worked, each kid would experience a life-transforming "God moment." Each room would have a special "real-life" plague experience. I confidently told one of our volunteers, "After this, the kids will *never* forget the plagues!"

I gathered up all the supplies I needed and trained the team. Finally, the day came for The Plagues Tour. I was really excited. I wanted to conduct the tour with the first group so I could see what it was like for the kids to enjoy the experience.

We entered the first room. The kids were amazed as they watched the illusion of clear water turning red, symbolizing the Nile River turning into blood. You should have heard the kids. Several of them said, "Wow! How'd they do that?"

I was getting really excited. This was the best idea I'd ever had!

We went to the next room that represented The Plague of Frogs. We had purchased hundreds of tiny plastic frogs from an online store and played a CD of frogs croaking. The kids loved it. They also enjoyed the next two rooms that had sound effects of flies and gnats. Things were going really well!

When the kids walked into the next room, they looked disgusted when they saw a dead cow—a fake one, of course. Oh well, all ten rooms can't be home runs. It was no big deal. The next room, though, wasn't exactly stimulating. We had a bunch of volunteers simulating the effects of The Plague of Boils. The leaders had done a great job with the theatrical makeup. The boils looked very realistic . . . apparently, they were a little too realistic. The kindergartners were terrified.

As soon as the doors opened, the boys started pelting the kids with ping-pong balls. Maybe, they'd played too many combat video games. They wanted to get lots of points, and they hit their targets!

Unfortunately, things kept spiraling out of control. In the next room, I'd made the mistake of putting some junior high boys in charge of The Plague of Hail. Several of them sat on the tops of ladders. They had hundreds of ping-pong balls in trash bags. I had very clearly instructed the boys to "lightly toss the ping-pong balls down on the children to simulate hail."

Is that what they did? Of course not! As soon as the doors opened, the boys started pelting the kids with ping-pong balls. Maybe, they'd played too many combat video games. They wanted to get lots of points, and they hit their targets! They smacked one of the girls in the eye. She was bawling, and the rest of the kids screamed and ran out of the room. I finally got the boys to stop throwing ping-pong balls, but by then, the kids were freaked out and crying.

The situation didn't improve through The Plague of Locusts and The Plague of Darkness. I guess I hadn't realized that many young children are actually scared of the dark. Go figure. But it all came to a final, disastrous end when we entered the last room on the tour—The Plague on the Firstborn.

One of our female leaders was dressed in full Egyptian costume with a baby doll in her lap. When the now, shell-shocked kids walked in, the leader screamed hysterically, "My baby is dead! My baby is dead!" The children ran out and didn't stop crying for twenty minutes.

In the chaos and crying, I had a stunning realization: My brilliant idea was a colossal failure. I ran back to the entrance, cancelled the remaining tours, and brought the kids down to the cafeteria for snacks. After all, a snack of cookies and Kool-Aid covers a multitude of sins—especially mine.

Needless to say, the next few days were very busy. I had meetings and phone calls from parents—some curious, some angry—wanting to know what in the world I was thinking when I came up with this idea. For some reason, the "God moments" explanation just didn't suffice for them. (Parents can be so unreasonable.)

My mistake: Thinking every good idea is a God idea.

Before the season of planning for Vacation Bible School, I'd spent a lot of time on my knees, seeking God's inspiration for ideas about reaching the children in my ministry. I asked Him for creative ideas, and God had answered. But a strange thing happened: As God answered my prayers for creativity, I began to think the ideas came simply because I'm a gifted, creative person. Hadn't I learned to ask, listen, and obey? Apparently not. If I had a good idea, I assumed it was a God idea.

Sometimes, we overestimate our own creativity and cleverness. We think we're so smart that we know exactly what we need to do in a given situation without consulting God. I had to learn the same lesson of trust again, but in a different way. Now, the problem wasn't my calling and role. I was foolishly depending on my God-given strengths instead of God himself.

In the Old Testament period of the judges, we find a man who made the same mistake. Samson met a beautiful Philistine girl in Timnah and decided to marry her. Before the wedding, he decided to throw a big, drunken party. Among those in attendance were thirty young Philistine men who were serving as Samson's groomsmen. At some point during the party, Samson decided to have a little fun with his groomsmen. He told them, "Let me tell you a riddle. If you can give me the answer within the seven days of the feast, I will give you thirty linen garments and thirty sets of clothes. If you can't tell me the answer, you must give me thirty linen garments and thirty sets of clothes" (Judges 14:12-13).

Samson thought he was very clever, but in reality, he was being an idiot. After all, there was only one of him and thirty of the other guys. They had a week to put their heads together and figure out this crazy riddle. And the wager wasn't wise, either. If the groomsmen lost, they owed Samson a single set of clothes, but if he lost, he had to come up with thirty.

It didn't turn out very well for Samson. His fiancée was a Philistine woman, so the men put pressure on her to find out the answer to the riddle. She decided to use her feminine charms on her man. When that didn't work, she used whining. After suffering through his fiancé's constant crying and nagging, Samson told her the answer to the riddle. Of course, she passed it on to the Philistine men, who announced the answer just before sundown on the seventh day. They won the bet and made Samson look like a complete fool.

It's a sad story. Samson tried to show how clever he was, but he was shamed in front of the enemies of Israel. If he had asked God for wisdom, the Lord would have surely kept him from making this huge mistake. Apparently, prayer never crossed his mind.

Although The Plagues Tour is the most entertaining and over-the-top story of overconfidence in my creative abilities, it's certainly not the only example in my life and career. In those early years of ministry, I didn't know what I didn't know. I lacked wisdom to spot a "God idea." Throughout my life, I've sometimes asked myself a haunting question: Why do I sometimes settle for good ideas instead of God ideas? Let me share a few reasons.

"I'm driven by pride."

Let's start with the one that hurts the most. Solomon described the impact of arrogance: "First pride, then the crash—the bigger the ego, the harder the fall" (Proverbs 16:18 The Message). In Samson's story, we can easily spot his pride. He believed he was much smarter than the Philistines. He planned to brag after he won the bet, but his pride caused him to overestimate his own ability.

How many times has pride caused us to rush into a situation because we feel compelled to prove who we are and what we can do? The desire to win applause and be on top causes spiritual blindness. We don't even see what we're doing. Pride is an enemy of wisdom.

—Pride keeps you from asking for advice.

—Pride makes you think your way is the best way.

—Pride produces the wrong motive because you want to impress those around you.

—Pride keeps you from slowing down and hitting your knees to ask God for wisdom.

If you want to increase the "God ideas" in your life, confess the sin of pride and choose a path of humility.

If you want to increase the "God ideas" in your life, confess the sin of pride and choose a path of humility.

"I'm impatient."

Sometimes, we get in such a hurry to come up with an idea that we don't take time to "wait upon the Lord" and hear His whisper. We hate delays, and we think we have to have the answer to the issue right now!

—Impatience is a product of stress, and it produces even more stress.

—Impatience makes people around us feel neglected or used because our time seems more important than them.

—Impatience in dating causes people to cross the line sexually.

—Impatience is the result of our failure to trust in God's goodness and greatness.

—Impatience is what causes us to implement a "good idea" instead of waiting on a "God idea."

Our culture breeds impatience. Most of us have memories of feeling impatient from our earliest years. You remember how you felt at Christmas, don't you? You begged your parents every day to let you open a present, days (or even weeks) before Christmas. You couldn't wait to find out what was in those pretty packages.

I have to admit that I'm not very patient. I'm one of those people who stand at the microwave tapping his foot, wondering why the two minutes to cook a burrito is going by so slowly!

I hate to wait in traffic. I like to move fast. When I'm driving on the highway, I really move fast. When one lane starts to slow down, I switch to the one that looks most promising. Then I switch back. I can't stand it if someone who is next to me pulls ahead (but maybe this is more of a pride thing than impatience).

Airports, doctors' offices, emergency rooms, and high school graduations—I hate them all. Actually, I don't know very many people who are content with waiting. If I find some, I need to hang around them so their attitude will rub off on me.

Too often, we're impatient with the process of receiving a "God idea." He may want us to slow down so we can pursue Him, listen to Him, and have our ideas pruned and shaped. But all this takes time. Impatience causes many of us to miss out on the "God ideas" that could advance our ministry and inspire our hearts.

"I fail to appreciate God's limitless creativity."

Even the most creative minds are finite. The term finite means "having bounds or limits; not infinite; measurable." But God is infinite. He is "far above all," not limited by any boundaries at all. When we draw only on our own creative resources, it's like drinking from a thimble instead of the Great Lakes. God's power, love, and plans are beyond anything we can imagine. If we cultivate an attentive heart, we'll tap into His limitless capacity. We'll never come close to the depths of His greatness, but we can take several steps closer! In his beautiful prayer in his letter to the Ephesians, Paul prayed, "Now to him who is able to do immeasurably more than all we ask or imagine, according to his power that is at work within us" (Ephesians 3:20).

What's the biggest dream you can imagine about how God can use you in his kingdom? Seriously, take a moment and think about it. Got it? Guess what. You just undercut God. Your greatest and grandest ideas don't compare to God's limitless plans and resources. God is not limited to working with our imagination. He goes well beyond it—immeasurably beyond.

Far too often, we forget the power of God to inspire us. We think His power is reserved for healings, conversions, and deliverances, but it also operates in our plans and dreams. God wants to inspire us with so many "God ideas" that we'll never be able to implement them all. But first, we have to have open, receptive hearts.

"I settle for man's ideas."

When I attended the Hell House outreach, I was amazed. It was definitely a "God idea" for that church and that setting. I know the pastor personally. He and his team sought God for years before they ever implemented the idea. On the other hand, I didn't seek God for one minute about The Plagues Tour. I saw what was working in one church and decided I'd adopt their idea, tweak it, and make it my own.

This phenomenon happens quite often in the church world. We go to a conference, attend a seminar, watch a youtube video, or read a blog as someone shares a great concept or strategy. We think, *What an amazing idea!* Then we run straight back to our church and try to duplicate it. We hear reports of what God is doing in the church down the street or the "hot church" in our denomination, and we try to chase their ideas instead of asking God for His ideas. We do this for a lot of reasons, including the fact that it's a lot easier to adopt someone else's "good idea" than invest time seeking a "God idea."

It doesn't take any time at all to get plenty of cool ideas from church leaders in every kind of ministry. Type the words "church growth ideas" on your browser, and you'll get over 2 million hits. There are books upon books and conferences upon conferences that provide a ton of great ideas. Don't get me wrong. There's absolutely nothing wrong with getting a good idea from someone. I'm a firm believer in attending conferences, networking with other ministries, and reading great books. However, books and conferences can easily become a substitute for seeking God and trusting Him for guidance and creativity.

I'm a firm believer in attending conferences, networking with other ministries, and reading great books. However, books and conferences can easily become a substitute for seeking God and trusting Him for guidance and creativity.

Jesus told His followers, "But seek first his kingdom and his righteousness, and all these things will be given to you as well" (Matthew 6:33). What do we "seek first"? Is it conferences, books, message boards, and ministry networks, and then do we go to God only when all those things begin to lose their punch? Instead, we should begin on our knees, seeking for His idea that will change our lives and ministry.

Many of us have been trying to figure things out on our own. We've bought into the idea that our clever schemes, brilliant problem-solving abilities, and creative ideas alone are actually working for us. If we were honest, we'd probably admit that we're not where we want to be. We've let all these good ideas crowd out the God-inspired ideas. Our hearts know the difference.

Six Questions

I wish I could give you a list of "Ten Ways to Discover God's Idea for Your Life and Ministry," but God speaks to different people in different ways.

God spoke to Moses through a burning bush.

God spoke to Samuel in an audible voice in the middle of the night.

God spoke to Joseph in a dream.

God spoke to David through the prophet, Nathan.

God spoke to Mary through the angel, Gabriel.

God speaks to people when and how He chooses, but let me give you a series of questions that can help clarify your thinking:

1. "Have I prayed about it?"

James, the half-brother of Jesus, gave us a pretty cool promise: "If any of you lacks wisdom, he should ask God, who gives generously to all without finding fault, and it will be given to him" (James 1:5). If the idea you're chasing came from any source other than a time of prayer, hit your knees immediately and ask, "God, is this your idea for my life and ministry?"

God's not trying to hide His will from you, and He's not trying to make you figure it all out on your own. He wants to give you wisdom and reveal His plan to you. He wants to give you incredible, amazing, God-inspired ideas. Pray about it. Ask Him for wisdom and clarity. He'll answer and show you the way.

2. "What does my pastor think about the idea?"

As early as possible, run your idea by your pastor or kids' ministry leader to get feedback and input. Take this step before you invest too much time and energy in your idea. Your pastor may be aware of liability issues or other reasons why your plan just won't work. Trust your pastor's judgment—he's been down this road before.

Take the initiative to make the appointment with your pastor or ministry leader. Explain the idea, including the pros and cons. If he approves it, that's wonderful. If he finds problems with it, then the conversation will save you a great deal of wasted time and embarrassment. (I can't tell you how much my pastor has saved me from all kinds of heartaches.) And talking with this person *before* you implement the plan builds trust for the future, too.

3. *"Does the idea resonate with the hearts of my team?"*

After your pastor gives you the go-ahead, consult with your ministry team. These people have the same passion as yours to impact the lives of the children in your church and community. Share the plan with them while your idea is still in its early stages. Don't wait until you have the entire strategy fleshed out before you bring it to the team for feedback. The longer you work on an idea before you present it, the less likely you're going to be willing to change course. If leaders develop a plan too far before they talk to their teams, they can become emotionally invested in an idea and refuse to listen to any suggestions. When they don't listen to their team members, trust erodes.

I remember when I thought I had a great idea for a Halloween outreach. I wanted to call it "The Candy Factory." It was going to provide a full array of experiences, entertainment, fun, and best of all . . . candy! I worked on the idea for weeks and weeks before I brought it to the team. When I finally presented it to them, they immediately had questions about it. They questioned the plans, the schedule, the execution, and the very idea itself. I became defensive. I'd worked several weeks on it, and this was my baby! How dare they question an idea in which I had invested so much time!

If the members of your team—the people whose hearts are aligned with yours and who care as much about kids as you do—believe the idea stinks, you better listen to them.

4. "Do I have the support of the parents in my ministry?"

This question applies especially to those who are young in ministry and have no children of their own. It is easy for young singles or couples without kids to miss red flags that are obvious to parents. Checking with them before an event can save you lots of headaches in the long run.

If I'd taken a few minutes to talk to parents before the infamous Easter Egg Hunt, they would have told me that it's inappropriate to have Atomic Fireballs and jawbreakers in plastic eggs on steep hillsides with big rocks for an event for preschoolers (or anyone else for that matter). They would have spoken up. They would have told me the hard, cold truth, and I would have seen that it was an idiotic idea to hold a preschool egg hunt on Drainage Ditch Hill. Parents would have looked me in the eye and told me, "Pastor Brian, the children will choke on those Atomic Fireballs. Are you insane?"

But it didn't cross my mind to ask any of the parents. Solomon advises us (me especially), "With many counselors, there is safety" (Proverbs 11:14 NLT).

5. "Do I need God's power to accomplish this idea?"

This is perhaps the most important question to ask yourself as you evaluate whether the idea is a "God idea" or just another good idea. If you can accomplish the plan without God's power and without God's anointing, it's probably not His idea.

God's ideas always require God's ability. If you can do it on your own, go back to the Lord and ask Him for direction. This doesn't mean that every impossible, crazy idea is necessarily from God. That's the wrong conclusion! We need to have a balance of wisdom and faith—it's not one or the other; both are required for good leadership.

6. *"If this idea succeeds, who will get the glory?"*

As I planned The Plagues Tour, I was thinking, *Man, when this thing is a huge success, people are going to think I'm the smartest guy around. Other children's pastors are going to ask me for my planning notebook so they can pull off their own Plagues Tour. This is going to rock!*

My plan to take all the credit for success was a clear indication that it wasn't a "God idea" at all. When people have trusted God for an idea, a plan, and success, they realize God is the source of every good thing, and he deserves the credit. Pursue God's ideas, and be prepared to give Him the glory. After all, He's the originator, not you. He's the creator, not you. He is the author and finisher, not you. He deserves the glory, not you.

Pursue God's ideas, and be prepared to give Him the glory. After all, He's the originator, not you. He's the creator, not you. He is the author and finisher, not you. He deserves the glory, not you.

I'm afraid I learn the best lessons the hard way. It took the disaster of The Plagues Tour for me to begin asking the six questions that help me determine if an idea is God's plan. Failure isn't the end of the world—unless we fail to learn from it. Over time, I've gradually figured out that every wild and crazy idea that comes into my head isn't necessarily from the Lord. I need to be patient and discerning, and I've learned to ask the six questions. But I've also realized that God's plans often are far beyond anything I can imagine. This doesn't give me license to go off and do something crazy. I still ask the same questions and look for feedback from people I trust. We're all in this together.

We don't have to settle for mediocre visions and mundane plans. Some of us have missed out way too long. We need to quit trying to make sense of God. We need to pray, listen, and respond in faith. We don't need to settle for just a good idea. We need to go for broke with thrilling, faith-stretching "God ideas."

Think about it...

1. What are similarities and differences between a good idea and a "God idea"?

2. What is the most common reason you settle for good ideas?

3. Which of the six questions seems most helpful to you at this point? What difference will it make?

4. Do God's plans always defy human logic? If not, how can you tell if you're settling for comfortable plans or reaching for faith-stretching ones?

"There's a Keystone Cop at Jesus' tomb!"

3

If you're a leader in a children's ministry, you know the need for anyone working with kids to have a lively sense of humor. The ability to make kids laugh is a huge asset. I've always felt that working with kids keeps you young because you have to stay sharp and witty to connect with kids.

But we can easily be misunderstood. We sometimes wear weird ties and mismatched tennis shoes, sing crazy songs, and act goofy. Our penchant for goofiness can cause some adults to be suspicious of our choices, our behavior, and our sanity—especially if we don't choose the right time to use it.

In 2003, I was chosen to be the narrator in our church's Easter production. In every church in the world, Easter is the most important service of the year. People who haven't attended church all year come that day. That weekend, thousands of people attended our four performances. I told the story of Jesus through the eyes of Nicodemus. To prepare for the event, I had grown a full beard and dressed in full Biblical costume. (I looked pretty fantastic if you want my objective opinion.)

In the middle of the final production, when Jesus was arrested, tried, and crucified, I left the stage for about 15 minutes because I didn't have any lines. During this interval, I wanted to go to our Media Production Room to watch the production on the television monitors. On my way there, I passed by our prop room and noticed a Keystone Cop hat we had used in one of our productions that year. I thought it would be funny to put that hat on and walk into the Media Room where several members of our other staff were gathered.

I was right. When I walked into the Media Room with the tall, pointed hat on my head, I got big laughs. I left it on while I watched the Easter play on the monitor. Suddenly, I realized I was hearing the line that was my cue to walk onstage. I rushed out of the Media Room and sprinted to the stage to deliver my lines. It was a pivotal point of the production: Joseph of Arimethea and Nicodemus were carrying the body of Jesus to the tomb.

I began to deliver my lines: "Joseph of Arimethea placed the body of Jesus in Joseph's own tomb . . ." At that moment, I noticed that Michael Winslow, the drummer in the orchestra, was looking at me with a strange expression. The orchestra pit was directly in front of the stage where I was standing, so I couldn't help but notice his stare. I don't read minds very well, so I had no idea what he was thinking. I could tell something wasn't right, but I kept speaking my lines. I recited, "The disciples were distraught. What had happened? One minute their Savior was entering triumphantly into Jerusalem, and the next minute, He was laying dead in a borrowed tomb."

I looked down. Michael was still staring at me, but now, his mouth was open and his eyebrows were furrowed in disgust. I was a little irritated with him. I was certain I was saying my lines perfectly. After all, this was our fourth performance, and I had them down pat.

About a minute into my lines, it hit me. I thought, *Oh, no!* I looked up out of the corner of my eye at the video screen on the wall. It revealed exactly what Michael—and everyone else in the congregation—was seeing. I

The moment after I looked up at the screen.

was still wearing the Keystone Cop hat! I was mortified, but I kept right on delivering my lines. I thought about taking it off, but that would have called even more attention to it. I thought about running off stage, but I had to finish. I couldn't just quit.

Somehow, I was able to finish my lines without breaking character. I got off the stage as quickly as possible. In leaving, I had to walk down a wooden plank and turn to my left, passing directly in front of Pastor Rod. I hoped he hadn't noticed, but the look on his face was unmistakable. I took one step at a time, and each one seemed like an eternity. As I walked past him, I whispered, "I'm so sorry. It was an accident." He had no discernable reaction. (I wasn't sure if that was a good sign or not.)

When I got out the door and walked into the hall, our Senior High Pastor, John Van Pay, and our Jr. High Pastor, Steve Flores, who had been watching on the monitors in the Media Room, met me. The look on their faces was a blend of sheer delight and deep compassion for my predicament. John stifled a laugh and asked, "Bro, how could you go out there with that hat on?"

I tried to come up with a good explanation, but all I could say was, "I forgot! I had no idea it was on my head until halfway through my lines." I was mortified.

To make sure Pastor Rod knew it was an accident, I scribbled a note to him that read, "I'm so sorry. It was an accident. I had no idea that hat was still on my head. Please, forgive me." I sent Steve to deliver the note as I watched from a cracked door in the back of the auditorium. I watched Pastor Rod open the note, read it, then fold it back up and place it to his side. Again, there was no reaction.

I knew I was going to be fired. I'd come out with a Keystone Cop hat on my head in the middle of Jesus being placed in the tomb. Who recovers from that? I was sick to my stomach.

After the crowd left the church, I found Pastor Rod backstage. I begged his forgiveness and promised him it was an accident and that I would never have deliberately come out on stage looking like that. He asked, "How did the hat get on your head in the first place?"

I had to admit my foolishness and responded, "I was trying to make John and Steve laugh in the Media Room. I shouldn't have done that. I apologize."

Pastor Rod is a very forgiving person. Although I'm sure there was plenty of doubt in his mind about whether I pulled this stunt on purpose, he forgave me for my stupid blunder. If the story had ended at that point, things would have been fine. The problem is, the saga continued.

I couldn't wait to get to the Media Room where our Media Director, Chris Lesher, was shutting down all the recording equipment. He laughed at me and told me how stupid I looked (as if I didn't know). I had an idea. I told him, "Chris, you have to rewind that and let me see it!" Chris rewound the tape and replayed the moment where I looked up at the screen and saw the Keystone Cop hat on my head. It was a priceless look. I almost fell over laughing at myself.

The commotion drew a lot of attention. Others came into the Media Room and asked Chris to rewind the tape so they could watch it, too. Before I knew it, the entire Media Room was filled with church staff and members of the congregation watching my idiotic blunder. We were all laughing hysterically, and I was the loudest of them all.

As we watched for about the eighth time, I caught the eye of Pastor Rod as he stood in the door of the Media Room. He couldn't believe that only minutes after I had given him a heartfelt apology, I was laughing with a whole host of people about what I had done. As soon as my eye caught his, he turned and walked out.

I only thought I had been feeling sick before. Now, I knew I was going to be fired. I immediately left the Media Room and followed Pastor Rod downstairs into his office. I sat in the chair in front of his desk and said, "I'm sorry. I was wrong. What can I do to make it right?"

My cute little attempt at being funny with my friends had ruined a very important production and had caused people to question my wisdom and leadership. But the public blow to my reputation didn't compare to the devastation I felt at the moment Pastor Rod looked at me from across his desk and said, "Brian, I think you have so much potential for leadership at First Assembly. I would love to give you more opportunities to lead, but you tie my hands when you pull stunts like this." My heart sank. It was a mistake I'll never forget.

My mistake: Allowing my greatest strength to become my greatest liability.

My greatest strength in kids' ministry was my sense of humor. The children loved it, and the volunteers enjoyed it, too. I was able to play goofy characters like Skittles, the Candy Rapper, and a host of others. I was quick witted and funny. I could make the kids laugh at almost anything, but I had a problem: I allowed this strength to run wild and unrestrained, and it became my greatest liability. This can happen in all of our lives, and it doesn't just apply to the strength of humor.

—A person who is driven can work so hard chasing his vision that he leaves a trail of ruined relationships behind because people feel used. He may accomplish his goals, but he hurts people in the process.

—A person who is extremely relational can spend all her time socializing and seldom get any work done. She focuses on the person in front of her, but she often misses the big picture and kingdom goals.

—A person who has empathy and senses the pain of others can find himself "taking up the offenses" of others, taking sides, and causing discord and disunity. He may develop tunnel vision by focusing on the hurts of a few but fail to notice the opportunity to have an impact on the many.

—A person who is diligent to manage details may be determined to do things exactly right, but his perfectionism makes him rigid, judgmental and offensive. He never feels that his work is finished, and he never thinks yours is done, either.

—A person who has grand and glorious visions may be impatient with others who are slow to get on board.

Any strength or skill, when it is taken to an extreme and isn't tempered by wisdom and love, can become detrimental to the person, the team, and the organization. As the old saying goes, "Too much of even a good thing is still too much!" The solution isn't to deny or minimize the strength, but instead, to use it in the right context with the right motive. In addition, we need to learn to value the skills and traits that complement and balance our strengths. We can get into trouble when we rely too much on our own strengths.

Defining Our Identity

Paul's letter to the Romans is considered one of the most important in the Bible. It paints a clear and powerful picture of the grace of God and our response of joyful obedience. We often quote the pivotal point in the twelfth chapter. There, we respond to all the mercies Paul has described in the first eleven chapters by presenting our "bodies as a living sacrifice—holy and pleasing to God" (Romans 12:1). After this invitation, Paul gives several chapters of instructions about how to live according to God's mercies. He begins, "For by the grace given me I say to every one of you: Do not think of yourself more highly than you ought, but rather think of yourself with sober judgment,

That means we're to be objective about our strengths, realizing they are God-entrusted gifts. And we're to be equally objective about our weaknesses, knowing they show how much we need to depend on God for help.

in accordance with the faith God has distributed to each of you" (Romans 12:3).

To live a life of faith, we need to become skilled in self-examination. Our tendency is to think too highly or too lowly of ourselves, resulting in either pride or shame. And some of us can experience both emotions within only a few minutes! Paul tells us to think about ourselves with "sober judgment." That means we're to be objective about our strengths, realizing they are God-entrusted gifts. And we're to be equally objective about our weaknesses, knowing they show how much we need to depend on God for help. We're self-absorbed because we're so insecure, so we desperately try to prove ourselves, win approval, or hide from others. A healthy understanding of the grace of God fills the gaping hole in our souls with the love of Christ and solves the problem of radical insecurity. Humility isn't self-hatred, and it's not denying our strengths. In fact, humility isn't thinking less of yourself; it's thinking of yourself less.

When we respond to the grace of God and our hearts are full of His love, forgiveness, and acceptance, we don't have to show off, and we don't have to be ashamed of our abilities. We can accept our talents as wonderful gifts from God, hold them loosely, and sharpen them so we can honor God as much as possible. But we can also recognize there's a Mr. Hyde behind every Dr. Jekyll—a dark side that needs to be exposed and addressed. My humor is a God-given talent, but far too often, I used my humor to shine the spotlight of praise on me instead of God.

God's grace invites us to define our identity as chosen, adopted, beloved children of God. We may be good at one or a hundred things, but these talents no longer ultimately define who we are. When our identity is rooted in grace, we can use our talents to honor God, and we aren't defensive if we don't get the praise we think we deserve. It's a wonderful place to live!

A Sign

One of the surest signs that we're getting our identity from our strengths instead of Christ is the nagging and gnawing habit of comparison. We don't compare ourselves to everybody in the world—but only those who have similar talents as ours. Artists don't compare themselves to accountants. They see how they measure up to other painters, sculptors, and designers. Speakers compare themselves to other speakers, leaders to leaders, and rich people to rich people. Comparison inevitably results in feelings of superiority (arrogance) or inferiority (shame). It causes us to be critical of others instead of appreciating their abilities or critical of ourselves because we're sure we don't measure up.

When we get our identity from our strengths, we feel the need to force our talents at inappropriate times. That's what happened to me over and over again. When I walked into the Media Room during the Easter production, I picked up the Keystone Cop hat because I wanted a laugh—not for my friends' sake, but so their laughter would validate me. And after I had apologized to Pastor Rod for my foolishness on stage, I made exactly the same mistake by showing the rerun of my blunder. I was again the center of attention. The incredibly sobering thing is that I was looking for laughs at the moment in the story when Jesus was being taken to the tomb. The Lord of Glory had paid the ultimate price for our sins while I was dancing and laughing, wearing my stupid hat. I was saying, "Look at me! I'm really funny. Can't you tell?" Sad . . . very sad.

Because my identity was so wrapped up in being funny, I felt uncomfortable in situations when my humor couldn't wow people. That trait is not a good thing when a pastor has to preside at funerals, visit dying people and their families in the hospital, or comfort hurting people. I've tried to crack jokes at the most inappropriate moments. My humor also doesn't work in regular staff meetings when people are trying to get things done. Left unchecked, my strength is distracting and even destructive, and it causes me to do stupid things, which inevitably produces crushing shame. That shattering moment in Pastor Rod's office was a loud, clear, and grace-filled message that something had to change.

True Repentance

In the weeks and months after my meeting with Pastor Rod, I thought long and hard about my compulsion to win approval through humor. And that's what it was: a compulsion. I thought about many times when I had forced a joke or tried to impress people with a sarcastic comment. Most of the time, they had laughed, but I now realized they had probably walked away thinking, *That guy is such a jerk! What was he thinking? Why did he try to make people laugh when it was entirely inappropriate?* I had accomplished the opposite of my careful design to earn their approval.

During those weeks, I had to be careful to avoid a common pitfall that occurs when people face their failures. I felt myself falling into a deep pit of self-pity. I thought that if I felt bad enough, long enough, I'd be able to pay for my faults. But that's not repentance at all. True repentance is turning from sin to Christ, and it produces gratitude and holiness, not groveling and shame. Paul described the difference between repentance and shame in one of his letters to the Corinthians. In his first letter, he had gotten all over them for all kinds of sins: sexual promiscuity, arrogance, and favoritism, to name a few. Later, he received word that a particular person had experienced genuine repentance, and he was thrilled. He wrote, "I am happy, not because you were made sorry, but because your sorrow led you to repentance. For you became sorrowful as God intended and so were not harmed in any way by us. Godly sorrow brings repentance that leads to salvation and leaves no regret, but worldly sorrow brings death" (2 Corinthians 7:9-10). "Worldly sorrow" is a sense that we're so bad that only self-hatred can ever make things right. It may feel appropriate as a way to try to make up for our sin, but it crushes our spirit. In contrast, "godly sorrow" points us to Jesus, refreshes us as it reminds us of His forgiveness, and promises the hope of genuine change for the future. Shame looks at the past and cringes. It has little hope for the future. Repentance looks at the past and is deeply grateful for God's forgiveness, and it looks forward with hope and joy.

Pastor Rod is a wonderful pastor and a great friend. When we talked in his office that day, he spoke the truth to me, but without a hint of anger. I had ruined one of the most important services of our year, but he communicated that he was concerned about me, my walk with God, and my impact on others. I took his words to heart. At that moment, reality hit

I took his words to heart. At that moment, reality hit me fast and hard. I hadn't just excused my selfish, stupid humor in the past; I'd gloried in it.

me fast and hard. I hadn't just excused my selfish, stupid humor in the past; I'd gloried in it. Now, I saw it for what it was. My compulsion to be funny had hurt the man I had made a commitment to honor and serve. I had been sabotaging my ultimate goals in life: to honor God, serve my pastor, and have a positive impact on the people around me. Reality hit me hard, but facing it with honesty was absolutely necessary if I was going to change.

For a while, I saw my humor only as a flaw that had hurt people. Gradually, I was able to see it as strength again, but with a dark side that could easily ruin any conversation and any event. For the first time in my life, I became cautious about using humor. I began to ask God for wisdom in how and when to use it, and when I didn't sense His affirmation, I changed gears. That's a big deal for someone who saw every moment in every day as an opportunity to get a laugh!

I've had a lot of layers of pride and self-protection. The day I put on the Keystone Cop's hat was when God peeled one of the layers off, revealed a bit more of my heart, and invited me to take a step deeper into His grace. In fact, each of the mistakes I describe in this book is another layer God identified and peeled off. They weren't fun, but they were absolutely necessary. I had gloried in my ability to make people laugh, but I had used this gift in selfish, inappropriate ways. God used this event to show me that he wanted to be the focal point of my life and the delight of my heart. I'm a slow learner, but I was gradually getting the message.

In his letter to the Philippians, Paul wrote, "Let your moderation be known unto all men. The Lord is at hand" (Philippians 4:5 KJV). Paul didn't say, "Be sure people are impressed with your talents." Moderation isn't being bland and lifeless; it's being wise, temperate, and measured in all we do.

Why do we make choices to do the right thing for the right reasons? Because we live each moment in the presence of the God of the universe. He's watching, and He's rooting for us to respond to His grace with glad obedience. When we try to get our identity from our talents, we compare and feel inferior or superior. If people give us the applause we want, we appreciate them. If they don't, we resent them or ignore them. But when our identity is deeply rooted in the mercy of God, we find security, peace, joy, and wisdom. And we want to please Him with all our hearts.

Think about it...

1. How have you seen a person's greatest strength become a liability?

2. What are your God-given strengths? What is the dark side of each one?

3.   How would you define humility?

4.   What are the differences (in focus, feelings, and results) between "worldly sorrow" and "godly sorrow"?

5.   What are some lessons you can apply from this chapter?

"They're just kids." 4

In my first years as a kids' pastor, I loved my job. I taught kids how to worship God, love God, and love others. We explored important biblical principles like The Ten Commandments, the fruit of the Spirit, and the Golden Rule. I often said, "These children are the leaders of tomorrow and the church of the future!"

I was wrong.

Daniel Davis was a ten year-old kid in our ministry. A seemingly random conversation with him one day rocked my world. He was sharp, articulate, and outspoken . . . very outspoken. In fact, Daniel had never been someone to hold back his opinions and feelings. A couple of years earlier, when I had first become Kids Pastor, I found Daniel sitting out in the hallway. I'm not a psychologist, but I could tell he was mad. I asked, "What's wrong, Daniel?"

He replied, "I don't want to go back into Kids Church. I want to stay out here."

I patiently explained, "Well, Daniel, we definitely need you to come back into Kids Church. We have a lot of great things planned today." I could tell he wasn't convinced, so I asked, "Why don't you want to come in?"

Daniel looked up at me and said bluntly, "Because it's boring. You're not as fun as our last Kids Pastor, Richie Brown. You're boring."

That was my introduction to Daniel's piercing perception and brutal honesty. As we interacted many times over the next three years, I appreciated the fact that he always shot straight with me, but sometimes it was hard to swallow—especially when he was right.

By the time Daniel was ten, I realized I didn't have to beg him for his input. One day, Daniel and I were hanging out with some young adults who were part of our church's Master's Commission program. This program trained them to do the work of the ministry, lead their peers, and share the gospel with lost people. It was a powerful and effective training tool. That day, the students were talking about an outreach they were planning later that week. Daniel had been listening intently and noticed the excitement on the faces of these young men and women. He looked up at me and asked, "Why don't we have something like Master's Commission for kids?"

I kind of laughed as I answered, "Well, because you're just kids."

He looked straight into my eyes and announced, "Kids can be leaders, too, you know! We can lead other kids. We can even lead adults. A leader is someone who shows other people how to do what's right." He was a bulldog. He asked again, "Why can't we have a Young Master's Commission?"

I left Daniel and the students, and I went straight to my office. I sat in my chair with my head in my hands. Daniel's words haunted me: "Kids can be leaders, too, you know!" The problem is I didn't know that—or at least I didn't believe it—until that moment. A ten year-old boy's words hit me like a wrecking ball. I realized he was right, and I'd been so wrong. I asked God to forgive me for making one of the biggest mistakes of my life in Kids Ministry.

> Daniel's words haunted me: "Kids can be leaders, too, you know!" The problem is I didn't know that—or at least I didn't believe it—until that moment.

My mistake: Underestimating the potential of kids to change the world.

Before Daniel

It's not that my ministry philosophy had been evil and demonic; it was just shallow and incomplete. There was nothing sinister in our motives, but I had failed to grasp God's vision for our ministry. Let me outline our philosophy before Daniel's question shook up my world. Our operating principles were:

Kids' ministry is a lot of fun.

Kids are important to God.

Kids' ministry helps my pastor.

Kids' ministry builds the church.

Kids' ministry is good stewardship.

Let me explain each one and show how it was incomplete:

Kids' ministry is a lot of fun.

In every church around the globe, there's one thing you can always say about people who are involved in kids' ministry: We know how to have fun! We have to. Without creating a fun environment, you can't capture the attention of an ADHD first grader to teach him about the love of God. I love the games we get to play! Actually, I feel sorry for the people who lead all the other areas of ministry because we have far more fun than they do. Can you see your Senior Pastor calling up some volunteers from small groups, men's or women's ministries, parking attendants, or ushers to see how many Life Savers they can lick and stick on their faces in sixty seconds? Yeah! Me neither.

I love the creativity we employ in teaching kids. Object lessons, skits, puppet shows, gospel illusions, games . . . you name it and we do it! Can you see your Senior Pastor using a "change bag" magic trick to illustrate the way God takes away our sin when we ask Him? Nope, not going to happen.

I love the wacky songs we get to sing in kids' ministry! I grew up singing "Father Abraham" and "I'm In The Lord's Army," but now, we get to sing songs like "The Throw Up Song." (It goes, "I think I'm gonna throw up! I think I'm gonna throw up! I think I'm gonna throw up my hands and praise the Lord!") Even when we sing the modern worship songs like "Take It All" and "King of Majesty," we get to add motions, jump, dance, and act like crazy people. I love it!

When you're in kids' ministry, everything is fun—even when we take prayer requests. You never know what kids are going to say. For a kids' pastor or leader, prayer request time is when you get to hear all about everything that is going on in every family in your church. Of course, many of their parents would die if they knew their kids were telling everything that happens in their homes.

I'll never forget some of my early experiences with prayer requests. One Sunday, the son of one of our board members (some churches call them deacons) raised his hand to request prayer for his dad who wasn't feeling well enough to come to church that day. Being a concerned kids' pastor, I wanted to know more details so I could pray more specifically for him. The child stated without a hint of embarrassment, "Well, he said he didn't think he would be able to come and sit on the church pews because his hemorrhoids are acting up real bad." I was sorry I asked.

Another Sunday, the daughter of one of our single moms requested prayer for her mother. I asked, "What can we pray about for your mom?"

The little girl said, "She's been really depressed lately. She keeps going around the house moping and talking about how much she just needs a man!" Her mother would have been mortified!

Prayer requests aren't the only times when you get surprising revelations from kids. It can happen at the most unexpected moments. On the Sunday before Christmas, a mom and dad were bringing their son to Kids Church for the first time, and they asked if they could talk with me for a minute. They were concerned because their son, Garrison, was extremely nervous about making the move up from pre-school ministry. I assured them that I would connect him to several other kindergarteners and even have him sit by one of our leaders to help him feel more at ease. They thought this was a great idea.

That morning, I was teaching the story of the birth of Christ. My focus was on the fact that Jesus was more than just a baby. He was the King of Kings and Savior of the world. I asked the children to close their eyes and think about being there on the day He was born. I said, "Imagine you're standing in the middle of the stable. All of the shepherds are there. You're surrounded by all of the sheep, goats, and other animals. Mary and Joseph are kneeling next to the manger where the baby Jesus lays. You take a few steps forward and stand right in front of the manger. As you look down upon the King of Kings, the Son of God, the Savior of the world, what are you feeling? What do you want to do at that moment?"

I asked the kids to open their eyes, and suddenly, I saw a hand raised in the middle of the room. It was Garrison. A half hour ago, he had been afraid of his own shadow, but now, he couldn't wait to participate. I called on him, "Yes, Garrison?"

He proclaimed, "Teacher, you know what I was thinking just now while we were pretending we were in the stable?"

I was sure he was about to share about the warm feelings of love and worship that he was feeling for Jesus. I couldn't wait for him to share with all the other kids. I said, "No, Garrison, what were you thinking?"

He replied, "I was thinking of a camel pooping!"

He replied, "I was thinking of a camel pooping!"

That sent the entire room in a fit of laughter that took minutes to calm down.

Those types of moments make kids' ministry totally unpredictable and thoroughly memorable. Kids aren't inhibited like adults. They know how to laugh, shout, jump, and dance without reservation or self-doubt. Before my conversation with Daniel, I had a firm belief that kids' ministry was a whole lot of fun. It certainly is, but it's a lot more than that.

Kids are important to God.

In each of the gospels, we find Jesus pouring himself into the lives of children. Many times, the disciples and religious leaders tried to chase the kids away and pull Jesus back into "real" ministry. But Jesus corrected them: "Let the children come to me, do not forbid them, for the Kingdom of Heaven belongs to such as these" (Matthew 19:14). Even when crowds of people gathered around Jesus to be touched and healed, He stopped to lay hands on children, hold them in His arms, and bless them. We sing "Jesus

Loves The Little Children" for a reason. Throughout Scripture, it's very clear that God values children much more than the adults do—especially the religious leaders, but also the disciples. Jesus warned them, "If one of these little children believes in me, and someone causes that child to sin, it would be better for that person to have a large stone tied around his neck and be drowned in the sea" (Mark 9:42). Jesus was serious about protecting, loving, and nurturing children.

In the culture of first century Palestine, people considered children to be a nuisance, but Jesus recognized the value of each child. He knows that there is more to children than just their playful nature and innocence. Inside each one is the soul that's precious to the Father. When I speak to parents and other adults, I often challenge them with these words: "Whatever is important to God should be important to you. Do your actions demonstrate that you believe children are important to God?" I encourage adults to ask themselves:

—Is my schedule too full to take time to show love to a child?

—Am I too busy with "real" ministry to get involved in training children in God's Word and ways?

—When I see a hurting child in the hallway, do I stop and put my arm around him or her, or do I just keep going?

It doesn't take a "special calling" to demonstrate God's love to a child. If we're truly Christ's followers, His priorities become our priorities, and the things that break His heart break ours. Children are important to God, and they should be important to each of us.

Kids' ministry helps my pastor.

An effective ministry to children has a positive impact on every person in the church. Parents are free to focus on their own spiritual growth, and members of the church staff don't have to worry about distractions in their classes, services, and other programs. It's difficult for most of us to pay attention in a room full of crying babies, squirming toddlers, and inquisitive kids.

Early in my career as a kids' pastor, I realized I was helping my pastor by providing a safe, secure, and secluded environment for children so that he could address important issues with the adults in our church. Distractions can ruin teachable moments. I believed I was serving him by providing an effective and entertaining ministry for children.

Kids' ministry builds the church.

When I began to see great things happening in our ministry, I noticed an amazing byproduct. The more kids got excited about coming, the more the parents were willing to bring them. I saw children who had come for the first time run out to greet their parents shouting, "I want to come back here next week. Can we? Please, can we?" Many families were added to our church because the parents were choosing a church based on the quality of the ministry to their kids.

The concept of using kids to attract their parents isn't new. McDonald's was one of the first companies in America to market specifically to kids. The company built playgrounds, invented a cartoon character as a pitchman, and gave prizes away in every kid's meal. Is it any wonder that it quickly became one of the leading restaurant chains in the world? The fast-food world had plenty of options, but millions of children begged their parents, "Can we *please* go to McDonald's?" Their enthusiasm wasn't because they loved the saltiness of McDonald's fries or the way the chicken nuggets were cooked. It was because McDonald's was tons of fun!

As I began to notice how parents were choosing a church on their kids' preferences, we began to develop a more intentional strategy. We planned outreaches designed for kids to invite their parents, and we made these events fun for everybody. In addition, our church established a presence in the community by launching a charter school. It was a public school that met on the church campus, not a private Christian school. Under state mandates, we couldn't talk to the kids about Jesus during the day, so we got creative. Our Kids Ministry started an after-school program called "PowerHouse." Every day, we had a wide range of fun and creative activities. We had crafts, snacks, and games, and we told them about our Kids Church. We assured them they'd love it if they came back on Sunday morning. We said, "I'm glad you're having fun. If you want to experience something amazing, get your parents to bring you to church on Sunday. We do even more great stuff then!"

Week after week, kids went home and begged their parents to take them to church, and many of them came. The parents and the kids came and gave their hearts to the Lord. As a result, the church grew. Our Kids Ministry was directly involved in building the church. Many churches miss the opportunities to reach out into the community by capturing kids' hearts. A strong kids' ministry can build the church. A leading pastor observes:

> Children's ministry will increasingly become an entry point, and
> in many cases *the* entry point into a church. Families will make

church decisions solely on the basis of their children. The trend used to be: Reach the parents and get the children. The trend now is: Reach the children and get the parents. In many cases, Senior Pastors will be the last to realize this strategic switch. The lack of an effective children's ministry will be the last, dying gasp as a church passes into irrelevance.[1]

Kids' ministry is good stewardship.

God has entrusted to each of us a certain amount of time, money, and talent. What we do with these resources is called *stewardship*, which is the "wise investment of resources in order to reach the maximum amount of return." George Barna, the nation's leading church demographer, found an astonishing fact while doing research on evangelism. He writes:

> We discovered that the probability of someone embracing Jesus as his or her Savior was 32 percent for those between the ages of 5 and 12; 4 percent for those in the 13- to 18-age range; and 6 percent for people 19 and older. In other words, if people do not embrace Jesus Christ as their Savior before they reach their teenage years, the chance of their do so at all is slim.[2]

This means children are one of the largest, most strategic, and responsive mission fields in America today. Many churches are investing far more time and money in trying to reach adults and teens than they are children. This plan doesn't seem like good stewardship.

> This means children are one of the largest, most strategic, and responsive mission fields in America today.

Imagine having $1000 to invest in mutual funds. Your financial advisor does his research and tells you that if you put your money in Fund A, you'll get a 32% return. But if you put your money into Fund B, you'll get a 4% return. And if you put your money into Fund C, you will get a 6% return on your investment. Which fund would you choose? Only a fool would put his money into the fund that is going to yield the smallest return. This, though, is the spiritual investment strategy of many churches in America. They put their time, money, and resources into the adults and teens, while giving the kids' ministry only token resources.

Don't get me wrong. I'm not saying, "Forget about teens and adults." Those ministries are vitally important. I was saved as a fifteen-year-old kid. I have a daughter, Ashton, who is in junior high and a son, Jordan, who will be in junior high in another year. I understand the importance of a strong student ministry. From a standpoint of wise stewardship, however, the largest harvest of souls for our investment is going to come from investing in children. Let's be wise in our investment into the kingdom. Let's give our kids' ministries the focus, attention, and resources they need to do an effective job of communicating the gospel to the largest and most fertile mission field in the world!

I'm very thankful that both of the churches where I've served understand the importance of investing in children. As they've poured resources into kids' ministry, we've seen a harvest of souls come into the kingdom of God.

After Daniel

All of these elements of a strategy for ministering to children are good, right, and valid, but they aren't enough. God used my conversation with

Daniel to broaden my vision and deepen my passion to train kids to be leaders today. In my office that day, I took out a piece of paper and wrote "Young MC" for Young Master's Commission. (Yes, I thought of the 80s rapper and his song, "Bust a Move," but that's beside the point.) These few words on a sheet of paper were the beginning of a planning process to equip kids to become effective leaders. It was to become one of the most thrilling experiences of my life.

A few days later, I found Daniel and told him how God had used him to redirect our philosophy and plans. He was blown away that I had listened to him. He promised to help me recruit the first Young MC team. We began with three people: Daniel, Stephanie Stewart, and Jonathan Powell. During four weeks in the summer, I led them as they prayed for an hour each day, read the books of Acts and Proverbs, memorized three passages each week, conducted several evangelistic outreaches, served in Kids Church, worked together at Kids Camp, and ministered during Sunday night worship services. In only four weeks, we saw incredible growth in the lives of those kids. They began to lead in passionate worship. They served joyfully and tirelessly. Many adults told me they were challenged to go further in their worship and service because of the example of these three kids. The kids weren't just leading other kids. They were leading the adults. Seeing them learn, grow, worship, and serve inspired me. Several times, I wondered why I hadn't seen it before. After all, God often used young people in magnificent ways.

The Bible includes a number of examples of children as leaders:

—Joash was crowned king as a seven-year-old boy. He later ordered the temple to be rebuilt after the exile so the people could worship God.

The narrator tells us, "All his life Joash did what was pleasing in the LORD's sight" (2 Kings 12:2).

—Samuel was a boy whose mother had dedicated him to the Lord. When he was a boy, serving Eli the priest in the temple, God shared His plan for the nation's future with him. The summary statement of Scripture about Samuel reads: "As Samuel grew up, the LORD was with him, and everything Samuel said was wise and helpful. All the people of Israel from one end of the land to the other knew that Samuel was confirmed as a prophet of the LORD" (1 Samuel 3:19-20).

—The young servant girl in the house of Naaman, the Syrian general, had the courage to speak up and tell her powerful master that the Lord's prophet could heal His disease of leprosy. She sent him to Elisha, and God performed a miracle (2 Kings 5).

—In the gospels, Jesus found a boy who had only a small sack lunch, but he offered it to Jesus to be part of feeding 5000 men (probably 20,000, including the women and children).

—When Jesus was only twelve, He astounded the teachers of the law when His parents took Him to the temple in Jerusalem.

God has, can, and will use children to change the world. They often have the simple faith that delights God's heart, and He responds by pouring out His blessings on them. God doesn't seem to be waiting on them to grow up and become "the future of the church." Children who have been saved by God's grace and filled with

God has, can, and will use children to change the world. They often have the simple faith that delights God's heart, and He responds by pouring out His blessings on them.

His power have the same anointing that adults have with the same experience. John Tasch, a children's evangelist, observes:

> A child doesn't have a Junior Holy Spirit while adults have a big Holy Spirit. It doesn't work that way. When God gives out His Spirit, He gives it without measure and without size. Children just need someone to train them to do the work of the ministry.[3]

I was at Oak Cliff Assembly when I encountered Daniel and we began Young MC. It grew each year and God used it to equip many kids. When I came to First Assembly of God in North Little Rock, Arkansas, in October 1999, I soon began a similar program called C.I.A., "Christians In Action." So far, over a hundred children have been trained for leadership and ministry in C.I.A. Young MC and C.I.A. were summer programs, but our children wanted year-round training. To meet this need, we developed F.B.I., "Fabulous Bible Investigators," a six-week course that teaches kids how to be servant leaders, read their Bibles, pray, share their faith, and make disciples.

When I stopped looking at children as the leaders of tomorrow and began to allow them to reach their potential to change the world, I was amazed at what God did through many of them. I could easily compile a book full of stories, but let me share just a few of them:

One of my pastor's sons, Parker, entered a contest and won a PlayStation and some games. He already had a PlayStation, so the Lord led him to donate the PlayStation and games to the Dorcas House, a home for battered women and their children. The children were thrilled when Parker arrived with the PlayStation, but he noticed their television didn't have the right connectors to hook it up. He decided to spend some of his savings to buy them a new television. Adults could learn a lot from this boy's display of sacrificial giving.

Rebecca Holland was a sixth grader who decided to run for class president. Her faith was strong, and she wanted to honor God in her nomination speech. She told students in her class:

> I think I would make a good president because I am not afraid to stand up for what I believe in, or for myself, or for someone else. I also think I would be a good president because I don't mind speaking in public. I also like to serve and help others. I believe the Bible is our guidebook for living. It is the written word of God instructing us how to live, and that all of it is 100% true. I believe that Jesus was born to a virgin in a stable in a manger. He grew up sinless, and then died on a cross to save us all, no matter what shape, size, or color. He rose again in three days and returned to heaven, and He is coming back. Until Jesus returns, I want to use the gifts God has given me to help others. Because of my relationship with Jesus, I am more joyful, loving, and serving. I will bring these qualities to the sixth grade as class president. I am ready to take the responsibility of becoming 6th grade president. Thank you!

Can you imagine giving a speech like that? Most adults wouldn't have the guts, but Rebecca's faith in God gave her boldness and confidence.

Spencer Dale was only seven years old when his little brother, Troy, severely burned his hand on the kitchen stove. Troy spent the whole morning crying. Their mom, Courtney, treated the burn and tried to console him, but Troy was in a lot of pain. Courtney described what happened:

When it was time to take Spencer to school, we got in the car. Troy was still crying. Spencer said, "Mommy please do something. He won't stop crying."

I said, "There is nothing to do. I've done everything I know to do."

That is when Spencer became smarter than me (for a moment). He said, "Mommy, let's pray. Jesus will heal him." We pulled over on the side of the street and prayed for Troy. We got to school, and I realized Troy had stopped crying completely.

I looked at Spencer and said, "He stopped crying!"

Spencer looked at me with tears running down his face and said, "I told you Mommy! Jesus can heal people!" Troy hasn't made a peep about his hand since.

When Braden Mitchell was in the fourth grade, his teacher gave the class an assignment to write a paper inviting "a famous person" to visit the class. Most kids would have written a famous athlete, musician, or actor, but not Braden. He wrote his paper to invite Jesus Christ to come to the class. Braden wrote:

I want to invite Jesus because He is loving, He died on the cross, He's the I am, He cares about us, He hears us, and He's the most powerful man to ever exist.

The first reason I would like to meet Him is He's loving. He is so loving He came to earth in the shape of a child for us. To help us be better people. That's why He's loving.

The second reason is because He died on the cross. He died on the cross for us so we could not go to [hell]. He suffered so we could be forgiven. That's why He died.

The third reason is He's the I am. The all knowing. The great one forever. I love Him so much. 'Excuse me if I cry.' That is how He is the I am.

The fourth reason is because He cares about us. In the Bible it said before He died He did two amazing things! When He figured out about dying on the cross, He prayed so hard He cried and sweated out blood! The second reason is because when He was on the cross being whipped, stabbed, and nailed by His hands and feet to the cross with a crown of thorns on His head which made Him bleed badly He said forgive them for they don't know what they're doing! He's amazing.

The fifth reason is because He heals. He heals the blind, the lame, and even the deaf. He is so awesome.

The last reason is He's powerful. So powerful He could take out anything. He could do ANYTHING! I think that's cool!

Joshua Dudte was a typical boy in the third grade. He liked sports (He's a huge Dallas Cowboys fan, like me), he enjoyed hanging out with his friends, and he loved to run and play at recess. Joshua also loved to read his Bible. He carried his Bible to school and set it on his desk every single day.

His teacher, Ms. Bryant, noticed Joshua's Bible and asked him about it. Joshua often read his Bible to her. Ms. Bryant says, "I watched Joshua reading his Bible faithfully and encouraging his friends to do the same, and I could really see his love for Jesus and for his friends. He wanted to make sure of their future."

Joshua shared his faith with his friends every chance he got. He started a club called Bible Buddies with several of the friends that he had won to the Lord. During recess one day, Joshua began sharing with his friend, Ashton, about how much God loved him. Joshua tells the story: "I told Ashton about Jesus. I asked him to pray, and he became a Christian. Now, he's reading his Bible, and he's a better kid now that Jesus is in his heart."

I have seen countless examples of children going against their natural instincts of selfishness to give sacrificially to missions. When Madeline MacNamara was seven, she wanted to raise $100 to help plant a church in Madagascar. She washed cars, sold some of her toys on eBay, and even saved up all the money she got from the tooth fairy. A week before the offering was to be taken, she asked God that her loose tooth would hurry and fall out so that she could get that tooth fairy money for the offering for Madagascar.

Tiarra Hopper started a "Beads for Needs" campaign to raise money for missions when she was six. She bought string and beads in order to make necklaces and bracelets to sell to others.

Emily and Andrew Dippel, ages 10 and 8, started up "Paws For A Cause." They bought dozens of plain pet bowls and decorated them with markers and paints. They sold them to pet owners and gave all the money they raised to missions.

Morganne Jumper was desperate to raise money to build a school for one of our missionaries in Laos. She knew that many children would hear

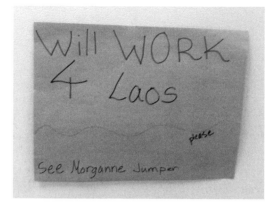

about the Lord if the missionary built the school. When school was out for a teacher-training day, most other children stayed at home watching television and playing games, but not Morganne. She went to work with her Dad and placed a hand-made sign on the refrigerator in the break room that said, "Will Work For Laos." She asked everyone for odd jobs so she could raise money for the school, and she made her goal!

Every week countless kids step up and do amazing things for God. Are they the church of tomorrow? Not hardly. They're the leaders of today! They inspire all of us through sacrificial giving, unashamed evangelism, and world-changing commitment.

Don't make the same mistake I did. Don't convince yourself that kids are important but not vital to the health and life of the church. They're world changers, and they'll blow your mind if you believe in them.

Even Me

Some people may read these stories of kids doing cool things and conclude, "Yeah, but we don't have any really sharp children in our church." Actually, God delights in using outcasts and misfits to accomplish His highest purposes. Kids who show little promise may not impress us, but if God captures their hearts, they'll do incredible things. I believe that with all my heart because I was one of those misfits.

Kids who show little promise may not impress us, but if God captures their hearts, they'll do incredible things. I believe that with all my heart because I was one of those misfits.

I was not exactly what you would call "prime material" to be one of God's servants. My parents were wonderful Christians. They made sure I was in church from the day I was born. My dad was a second-generation pastor, and my mother was a godly woman from a small town in Alabama. They did everything they knew how to raise me right and instill biblical principles in me.

But I was one of *those* kids. You know what I mean. I was a "church brat."

Every Sunday, schoolteachers cringed when they saw my name on their roll. I was an undiagnosed ADHDD, "Attention Deficit Hyperactive Disorder Deliberately." I had high energy, high impact, and was highly annoying.

I took joy in tormenting my Sunday school teachers. I interrupted

Me—six years old.

them, threw things, pulled chairs out from under other kids, and made it my mission in life to disrupt the class. In the first grade, I made my Sunday school teacher cry. In the third grade, I made my Sunday school teacher cuss. None of the other kids knew what the word meant, but I sure did. In the fourth grade, my family visited another church, and I went to Sunday school. In only a few minutes with me, the teacher lost her cool and slapped me across my face.

In the sixth grade, I forced not one, not two, but three Sunday school teachers to quit. The only person they could find to teach the class was my own grandmother. I made sure I behaved then because I knew Grandmother Taylor meant business!

During those difficult years (for my teachers, for my parents, and for me), one of the volunteers in our kids' ministry, Miss Candy, made a point of putting her arm around me every Sunday morning. She smiled sweetly and told me, "Brian, you're going to do great things for God." She had the eyes of faith because there was nothing obvious that would lead her to that optimistic conclusion. Her regular and sincere affirmations were seeds that sprouted much later when I realized she had been right all along.

When I was old enough to go to church camp, I regularly got saved and lived the Christian life for a couple of weeks. As soon as I went home and spent time with my friends, I was back to the same old selfish attitudes and destructive behaviors. But when the next summer camp rolled around, the process would begin again. Live like a sinner, go to camp, get saved, and fall away—it was a vicious cycle.

When I was 14, I went to church camp, determined I was not going to get saved. And I didn't. Each night, instead of going to the church services, I hid out in my dorm room, cranked up my Van Halen tapes, and waited until the service was over. My youth pastor, Brent Williams, was not happy with me. He told another youth pastor, "I have a demon in my youth group. His name is Brian Dollar."

I was always the strongest leader in the youth group, but I wasn't leading in the right direction. I was living for myself, and I was far from God. I was determined to be the worst sinner I could be. That is until February 26, 1989.

I distinctly remember that day. I was sitting in my parents' bedroom. They had found some evidence that my heart wasn't right with God, so they talked to me about my future, how much they loved me, and what God wanted to do with my life. I vividly remember the conversation. Tears of conviction slid down my cheeks. The Holy Spirit was drawing me to God. I knelt down at the side of the bed with my parents on a Sunday afternoon and asked Jesus to be my Lord and Savior.

I was thrilled and relieved! I couldn't wait to get to church that night so I could tell Brent. I walked up to him and announced, "Brent, I got saved today!"

He looked at me and said, "Brian, that's not something to joke about."

My youth pastor didn't believe me when I told him I'd become a Christian. That's how bad of a kid I was. But my salvation experience was real.

Over the next several years, God did some amazing things in my life. Pastor Brent took me under his wing and poured into my life, building me into the young man of God he always believed I could be. I was no longer the demon of the youth group. Instead, I helped lead worship, teach discipleship, and minister in outreaches. I never regretted my decision to follow Jesus, and I didn't turn back to my old way of life. I was in love with Jesus, and I wanted to please Him.

When I look at the faces of the kids in each class at our church, I try to look past the distracted stares and out-of-control behavior. I see kids who

Jesus loves with all His heart and who have the potential to change their world. They aren't nuisances. They're treasures. If God could work in my life, He can work in anyone's. Don't miss the heart of the gospel. Jesus came for outcasts and misfits. You have plenty of them in your kids' ministry. Some of them are just like me.

Think about it...

1. What might be some differences between a kids' ministry that sees children as the hope of the future and one that sees them as world changers today?

2. What strategies and programs might need to be implemented to equip kids to have the heart and skills to have an impact on their world?

3. How would this strategy affect your role and how your kids' ministry invests its resources?

4. What results would you expect?

5. Think of the kids who cause problems in your ministry. How would it help you if you saw them as people with incredible potential instead of nuisances?

"What do parents know about the Bible anyway?"

5

In my role as Kids Pastor, I gradually understood more about what makes kids tick. As I went deeper into their world, I was able to communicate more effectively and see lives changed. Many parents brought their children to me for spiritual guidance. For instance, a dad asked, "Johnny was asking me questions about baptism last night. Would you meet with him to explain what water baptism is all about?" I gladly took Johnny to my office, and I explained the important role that water baptism plays in the lives of believers.

On several occasions, parents cornered me after church and said, "Last night, my child asked me a bunch of questions about salvation. I think she's ready, but I don't know what to say. Can you talk with her about Christ and pray with her?"

I was excited to help. After all, I was the resident expert on children's spiritual needs. I was trained, and it was part of my spiritual DNA. I could communicate God's grace to them in a way that was clear and understandable. Slowly, I came to the conclusion that I was the go-to person to meet the spiritual needs of every kid in our community. I was filling a huge need, and it felt great. As my confidence grew, I concluded that parents aren't equipped to share deep spiritual truth to their children.

I was so wrong.

Two factors led me to the wrong conclusion about parents. First, people who minister to kids love what they do, and they feel great about the impact they have on kids. There's absolutely nothing sinful or evil about our passion for kids. We're doing what God has created us to do. Paul explained to the Ephesians that our ministry is God's gift to us as well as a responsibility for us to fulfill. He told them, "For we are God's handiwork, created in Christ Jesus to do good works, which God prepared in advance for us to do" (Ephesians 2:10). As we hone our skills and see God use us, we gain confidence and the sheer joy of seeing lives changed. The second factor is that a lot of the kids who come to us are from difficult home environments. Half of them come from broken homes, and many more get out of the car on Sunday morning to escape a poisonous atmosphere of cold resentment or hot bitterness—or both. Many dads are physically or emotionally absent, and many moms overcompensate by controlling and smothering their kids. Many of the children who walk through our doors desperately need a loving adult to step into their lives to demonstrate the grace, stability, and love of God. We wanted to be those adults.

We can respond to these factors in very opposite ways. We can develop a savior complex, believing that we are the only ones who can rescue a child from heartache and a dead-end life. When we have this perspective, we elevate our importance and deflate the role of parents—even the best of them. Or we can have a genuine

> We can develop a savior complex, believing that we are the only ones who can rescue a child from heartache and a dead-end life. When we have this perspective, we elevate our importance and deflate the role of parents—even the best of them. Or we can have a genuine sense of humility.

sense of humility. We recognize that God has given us an important role, but it never replaces the primary position of parents as the God-given leaders in these homes. Without realizing it, we can slip into a savior complex and unwittingly harm the most important relationship in the child's life. I came to an important conclusion: We aren't saviors. Our role is to complement and support the parents. After all, no matter how poorly they parent, they at least brought their kids to us so we could pour the love of Christ into them. We have to at least give them that.

I finally realized the error in my perspective when I had children of my own. When my daughter, Ashton, was a little girl, Cherith and I began reading the Bible to her and praying with her. She asked lots of questions, and we had wonderful conversations. As an expert in children and their spiritual development, I usually had pretty good answers. When I "put on my Kids Pastor hat," Ashton began to understand God's love in a very real way.

At one point Ashton asked, "Daddy, why did Jesus die on the cross?"

I was thrilled to hear her ask this question! To explain the gospel to her, I took off my "Daddy hat" and put on my "Kids Pastor hat." I told her about sin, its destruction, and the love of God that caused Him to send His Son to save people from their sins. After I had unraveled the mysteries of the spiritual universe, I put my "Daddy hat" back on.

I thought the ability to switch hats made me a superior parent because I was able to play both roles with my children: Daddy and Kids Pastor. When I prayed with Ashton and my son, Jordan, each night, I thought our prayers were very special because I was able to bring my Kids Pastor knowledge into our home.

Then, one night, it happened. I was praying with Ashton before she went to sleep. She looked up at me and said, "Daddy, can I ask Jesus into my heart?" I asked her a few questions to see if she understood the gospel of grace. Her answers showed me that she got it, so I led my daughter in the prayer of salvation.

It was an unbelievable experience! Cherith and I celebrated the amazing born-again experience of our daughter. I was on cloud nine! Over the next several days, I told everyone with ears about God giving me the privilege of leading my own daughter to the Lord. I was front and center for the biggest milestone in my child's life.

A few days later, a stunning thought hit me: *Wow! Parents don't know what they're missing. When they bring their kids to me to pray with them to receive Christ, they're missing out on one of the greatest experiences of their and their child's life.*

The thought led me to ask a simple question: "Why?"

—Why did parents bring their kids to me instead of praying with them on their own?

—Why didn't parents take the opportunity to answer their kids' spiritual questions?

—Why was it so easy for me to talk to my children about spiritual matters but seemingly so difficult for other parents?

These questions led me to others:

—Has it always been this way? What did parents do before there were kids' pastors?

—Other than training, knowledge, and confidence, what was the difference between those parents and me? Do I care more about their kids than they do? Surely not.

—Was I responsible for creating this gap by not equipping parents to lead their children in spiritual formation? (I wasn't sure I wanted to know the answer to this question.)

As I began to wrestle with these important questions, I began to feel convicted and guilty. I realized I'd made a huge mistake.

My mistake: Not recognizing the role of parents as the primary spiritual leaders of their children.

In the next few days, I came to the heart-wrenching conclusion that I had actually contributed to the problem by making myself the spiritual leader of the children in my Kids Ministry. My actions (and inaction on the part of training and equipping) had actually encouraged parents to abdicate their role as primary spiritual leaders of their kids. I began to study other kids' pastors and discovered that many of them had come to the same realization: God's plan is for parents to be the primary spiritual leaders of their children; our role is to support them and equip them.

In response, I made a commitment to honor the parents of every child who comes through our doors. I tell the kids that our ministry is here to support their parents, and I tell the parents we're here to serve them in every possible way. I don't want there to be any suspicion that we're trying to take the parents' role away from them. The parents who have been part of our church for a long time take this for granted, but those who are coming for the first time—and especially those who haven't been part of a church—need to be reassured that we're committed to serve them. In a dozen different ways, I tell the kids and the parents, "We're on the same team and are committed to the same purpose: to support your role as parents and encourage your child's spiritual growth."

Occasionally, a child will tell me, "I didn't come last week because my dad doesn't think it's important."

I ask, "Did your dad say that?"

Usually, the child will say, "Well, no, but since he didn't bring me, he must have something against me coming."

I quickly respond, "Wait a minute. We can't draw that conclusion. Give your dad a break. I'm sure he was just busy and couldn't make his schedule work out. After all, you're here now." I'm very careful to avoid relational triangles where two people gang up on another. In this case, I'm not willing to join the child in accusing his dad of wrong motives. It may seem like a small commitment, but I assure you, it's huge.

If a child's parents don't attend our church, come only occasionally, or aren't believers, we want to accomplish two objectives: honor the parents and equip the kid to be a soul winner in his family. Our message to the child is clear, intentional, and direct. I tell the kids, "God has put you in your family for a purpose. If you want your parents, brothers, and sisters to come to Christ, you have to show them the love of God in your actions as well as your words. You can't expect to win them to Jesus if you act like a selfish punk." They seem to understand this concept. Even first graders get the

We never want the kids to use church as leverage to blame and control their parents. Instead, we want to turn that upside down so they become loving, obedient, joyful lights that show their family members the grace of Christ.

picture that they can be lights in their families. They can let their light shine so their parents and siblings see Jesus in them. We never want the kids to use church as leverage to blame and control their parents. Instead, we want to turn that upside down so they become loving, obedient, joyful lights that show their family members the grace of Christ.

The Biblical Perspective

Let's face it: God created the institution of the family long before He created the church, and kids' ministry leaders came along even later. The first chapters of Genesis establish the family as the primary social unit under the leadership of God. Of course, those chapters also describe the fact that we chose to avoid God's rightful role in our lives. We rebelled and experienced the devastating consequences of sin, but God didn't leave us helpless and hopeless. His grace shines through even in our darkest moments. The role of parents is front and center in the process of reclaiming hearts. Moses told the people:

Only be careful, and watch yourselves closely so that you do not forget the things your eyes have seen or let them slip from your heart as long as you live. Teach them to your children and to their children after them. Remember the day you stood before the Lord your God at Horeb, when he said to me, "Assemble the people before me to hear my words so that they may learn to revere me as long as they live in the land and may teach them to their children" (Deuteronomy 4:9-10).

And he explained:

These commandments that I give you today are to be upon your hearts. Impress them on your children. Talk about them when you sit at home and when you walk along the road, when you lie down and when you get up. Tie them as symbols on your hands and bind them on your foreheads. Write them on the doorframes of your houses and on your gates (Deuteronomy 6:6-9).

Moses, Solomon, and Paul continued to explain the central role of parents in the spiritual nurturing of children (Deuteronomy 11:18-19, Proverbs 22:6, Ephesians 6:4, etc.). In the pages of Scripture, God has given parents the privilege and responsibility to shape their kids' spiritual lives.

Common Sense

Beyond the clear teaching of Scripture, good, common sense tells us that kids' ministers can't (and shouldn't try) to assume the parents' responsibility. We have about an hour a week with these kids, and we usually can't give any focused attention to an individual child. That hour is important for many reasons—including imparting spiritual truth, normalizing godly values, connecting kids to the church, and validating spiritual decisions—but we can't possibly give children everything they need to live a strong, effective, Christian life in an hour a week. In past decades, many kids' ministries had another hour with kids, but many churches today have cancelled Sunday night and midweek services. Kids' ministry leaders are losing time to influence kids, so the parents have an even more important role.

Parents get an average of more than 70 waking hours each week with their children. They may not actually use this time to connect in meaningful ways, but the time is there. I arrived at this figure by taking 168 hours in a week, subtracting eight hours of sleep per day (56 per week) and seven hours per day of school for five days. Of course, many kids are involved in extracurricular activities, but those are things we choose.

Many parents are very conscientious about the spiritual role they play in their kids' lives, but some struggle with this responsibility. Why? There are many different reasons. Shaping a son or daughter's spiritual life is difficult and demanding. It requires insight and determination. There are no guarantees that a child will respond with glowing gratitude to a parent's initiative. Many parents haven't been equipped to impart spiritual life to their kids. They may be doctors, lawyers, carpenters, or skilled in some other way, but a lot of parents feel completely incompetent in leading their kids spiritually. Sadly, the church hasn't done much to equip them.

To compound the problem, some kids' ministry leaders have gotten in the way of parents. A savior complex causes us to elevate our roles and look at parents as second class. When confidence becomes arrogance, we become a hindrance to God's grand plan. In addition, many churches have programmed the family worship experience out of existence by dividing up every age group and seldom (if ever) having the family together. In an effort to fill the void left by inadequate parenting, some kids' ministries have elbowed parents out of their roles as the primary spiritual leaders of their children.

Equipping Parents

Charles Spurgeon was one of the greatest preachers of the 19th century. In his book, *Spiritual Parenting*, he writes, "Children must be fed. They must be well fed, or instructed, because they are in danger of having their cravings perversely satisfied with error. The only way to keep chaff out of the child's cup is to fill it brimful with good wheat. The more the young are taught, the better; it will keep them from being misled."[1] Kids' ministries flourish only when a church has a comprehensive strategy to strengthen families. Let me offer some suggestions to reorder the universe so that kids' ministry leaders and parents play their God-given roles. Here are some things we've done to equip parents to spiritually nurture their kids:

—When parents bring a child to me and ask me to lead him to Christ, I explain to them the joyous opportunity they might be missing. I give them some pointers about how they can talk to their child about Christ and pray with him or her.

—We involve parents in water baptisms for their kids.

—We have a comprehensive strategy to strengthen families. We coordinate our kids' ministry efforts with the Sunday morning services, the small groups ministry, classes, concerts, seminars, and everything else. We don't have isolated silos; we work together for a common purpose.

—We coordinate the content for every age group in the church so we're all studying the same passages and learning similar lessons. This way, parents, children, and teenagers can have meaningful conversations about what they've heard in church.[2]

—We include a Family Devotion in the weekly bulletin to give parents a simple, clear tool to lead their children in a spiritual discussion based on Sunday's message.

—We conduct classes to train parents to talk to their kids about important topics, such as salvation, sex, drugs, friends, tragedy and loss, good decision-making, and death.

—We've designated every Sunday night as our "Family Service" so kids and their parents can worship together—and we don't worry about distractions.

—To elevate the importance of the parents' role, we've taught a number of sermon series on family dynamics, communication, forgiveness, understanding, and love. We come back to these important issues regularly and often.

In his research, George Barna discovers, "The more intentional a church is about giving parents the confidence and the tools to raise up spiritual champions, the more effective we found the congregation's parents to be as spiritual mentors."[3] We've become pretty intentional!

Advice for Parents

To give parents handles on the process of spiritual leadership in their homes, we offer some suggestions in our training, messages, and devotionals:

Pray with your kids daily.

Pray more than just at meals. Pray when they leave for school, when they go to bed, and when you or they face a difficult choice. Let prayer become part of the fabric of daily life. You don't have to pray grand, long prayers that sound like a preacher. Let them be simple, honest, and heartfelt. Prayer is simply talking to God and allowing Him to speak to you. That's the kind kids appreciate. As your kids see how much you value prayer, it will become part of their daily lives as well. You might want to use The Lord's Prayer as a guide, or you can use Paul's prayers in Colossians 1, Philippians 1, Ephesians 1 or Ephesians 3. Of course, the Psalms are prayers and songs to God.

Have regular family devotions with your kids.

As a family, read a passage in the Bible and discuss what it means. Allow the children to ask questions. It's okay to admit, "I don't know the answer to that. Let me find out so I can give you a good answer." Elevate the importance of the Bible. In our church, we often say, "The Bible is our guidebook for living."

Worship with your kids.

Kids need to see their parents praising God and responding to Him with honesty, joy, and gratitude. When a parent is excited about worshipping God, it's contagious. If the church doesn't provide a family worship service, parents can invite their children to attend the adult service with them once a month. Worship isn't restricted to church, though. Make it a part of the family devotions.

Serve with your kids.

Find an area of ministry where you all can serve together. As a family, join initiatives to feed the homeless, visit a nursing home, serve in the nursery, or give to missions. The opportunities to make a difference in your church and community are almost limitless. If nothing seems to grab your family members' hearts, go online to find other options. Some kids in our church have started ministries to meet specific needs. When God gives them a heart to help people in need and a vision to make a difference, watch out! It's an incredible thing to see. Compassion is more often caught than taught. Allow them to see the heart of Christ in you so they can pursue His purposes in their own lives.

Model godly behavior for your kids.

Too many moms and dads subscribe to the "Do as I say do, not as I do" philosophy of parenting. This is a disaster because it undermines their efforts to raise godly children. Leadership expert John Maxwell says, "We teach what we know, but we reproduce what we are."[4] Your kids will follow your example whether you like it or not.

Open Dialogue

An effective, comprehensive, church-wide strategy doesn't just happen. It's the product of many conversations, lots of prayer, and intentional planning. As a kids' ministry pastor or leader, you may already have worked out this kind of strategy with your pastor and other church staff. If not, take your pastor out to lunch and begin an open conversation about coordinating your kids' ministry with the rest of the church's activities. You might ask:

—What are your ideas about how our church can equip parents to be the spiritual leaders in their homes?

—What are some tools we can put in parents' hands for them to use with their kids?

> An effective, comprehensive, church-wide strategy doesn't just happen. It's the product of many conversations, lots of prayer, and intentional planning.

—How can we make a better connection between what the parents are getting in sermons and the children are hearing in kids' church? (We could at least let the parents know the topics we're teaching their kids.)

—How can we help parents understand how to talk about their spiritual lives in conversations with their kids? (Many children, and especially teenagers, are hesitant to talk about their own spiritual perceptions, so the parents can take the initiative to talk about what they're learning.)

—What kind of classes or seminars can we use to equip parents?

—What can I do to help you in formulating and implementing these plans? (Pastor, I'm certainly not trying to add to your workload!)

Your pastor may already have plenty of ideas about these issues, but he may be caught off guard by your questions. If you sense any resistance, back off a bit and share your heart about being a team player to accomplish the pastor's vision for the church. You certainly can assume that he wants parents to be equipped to be spiritual leaders in their families. Begin a long, constructive dialogue with your pastor and other church staff so that you're all on the same page, with one heart to reach people for Christ and help them grow in their faith. Kids' ministry is vital to this vision. Your pastor may not see it yet, but he will—if you communicate graciously and persistently.

It Makes a Difference

A couple of years ago, Ethan and Kristen started attending our church with their daughter, Lauren. They understood their responsibility was to "raise their daughter in church," which meant that they dropped her off and trusted us to make a difference in her life. They assumed waving to her as she walked in our door was the fulfillment of their responsibility. They didn't understand that being the spiritual leaders of the home meant they were to invite God into every aspect of their lives and relationships.

After coming for several months, Kristen saw the weekly devotions in our church's bulletin. She talked to Ethan about using them to talk to Lauren, and they decided to give it a try. They were amazed at how much of a difference it made. They began having rich, meaningful conversations with Lauren and each other about God's truth and His will for their lives. As each one drew closer to God, they grew closer to each other as well. With God in the center of their family's life, everything took on more spiritual significance. Lauren thrived in a home where her parents were growing in their love for God and for each other.

The shift in my perspective about the role of parents has made a difference to me, and it's had a big impact on our kids' ministry team, too. We no longer feel the rush of adrenaline or the crushing weight of responsibility of being saviors for the kids. We realize we're partners with the parents who bring their kids to us. Some of these mothers and fathers need help with their own pressing needs, but we don't condemn them for not being perfect parents. Our role is to love their kids and support the parents so they can become great moms and dads—and hopefully, lead their families spiritually. This is plenty of responsibility for us. And it's right.

Think about it...

1. Why does it feel so good to see ourselves as saviors of the kids in our ministries? What do we get from trying to be saviors of the children (and maybe the parents, too)?

2. What do we lose by trying to be saviors? How is over-responsibility damaging for us, for the kids, and for the parents?

3. What are some specific steps you can take to equip parents to be the spiritual leaders of their homes?

4. Who are some parents in your church who are great examples for others to follow?

"Hi ho, Silver!" 6

When I'd been involved in kids' ministry for six years, I was starting to hit on all cylinders. Our Sunday morning kids' services were going really well. My writing skills had improved. By this time, I was writing original skits and lessons for our Kids Church service called "Sonshine City." (By the way, this wasn't a good name. When some of our pastors tried to pronounce it too quickly, some of them accidentally cussed in the pulpit!) I was attending conferences so I could learn puppetry, illusions, object lessons, wacky games, and all kinds of other innovative activities.

The church at Oak Cliff was growing, and so was our Kids Ministry. With the addition of our charter school, many kids in the community were connecting to our church. They were getting saved and bringing their families. It was an exciting time, but the pressures steadily grew. It seemed that each week, I had to do more in less time. I'd never been good at managing my time, but I was forced to cram more into 24 hours every day.

As the pressure mounted, I tried to do all the work by myself. If you'd asked me if I was a control freak, I would have denied it. But any objective observer would have seen that I delegated less as the stress increased. I had several capable volunteers, but I rarely gave them any control or authority. I was determined to do things myself—so they'd be done right.

We were bursting at the seams, so I split our Sunday morning service into two age groups. We divided the kids into two groups: kindergarten through third graders and fourth through sixth graders. Even though having two services seemed logical and necessary, I was reluctant because it would mean I had to relinquish control of one of them.

Luckily (and because God was so good to me), I had met and married a smart, beautiful, and talented young lady earlier that year. Cherith had a passion for the younger group, and she had an amazing ability to communicate with volunteers, parents, and kids. She was high energy and loveable, so I knew she would thrive as the leader of Sonshine City. I didn't say it out loud, but since she was my wife, I knew I could keep a handle on her and this part of our ministry. I trusted her, but I sure didn't want to give up control!

I was the primary leader of the older group, called Young Warriors. I recruited some volunteers to help me with that service, but I was definitely the one calling the shots. I don't know why anyone would've said I was a control freak—just because I insisted on leading Young Warriors and running over to check on Cherith and Sonshine City several times every Sunday morning. After all, I was the Kids Pastor. It was my responsibility, and I had the most experience and training. I thought I was "the man" because I could juggle so much at the same time. (Actually, I was only juggling two balls, and even the worst juggler can do that.) Suddenly, however, things changed.

Our music pastor resigned his position, and our church began interviewing people to fill his role. During that time, we had no worship leader. Pastor Wilson asked me if I would be willing to step in and lead worship on Sundays. I love to lead worship, so I responded, "No problem. I'm glad to help."

After I agreed to lead worship, I realized I had a big problem. The worship service was, of course, at the same time as our two kids' church services. I scrambled to figure out how to be at three places at the same time! Each Sunday morning, I led the congregation in worship for about 15 or 20 minutes, and then I rushed out during the prayer time and headed upstairs to Sonshine City. I made a grand entrance and told some wacky jokes to make them laugh, and then I sprinted down to the Young Warriors where I preached the message. I kept close track of the time. I had to leave so I could get back into the sanctuary for the closing song and altar time.

Does this sound totally insane? (Don't answer that question.) I thought this was a thoroughly reasonable and workable plan. But there was one more complication: I was also the media/video director for the church. I produced video projects every week for the regular worship service and the student ministry. And of course, all of this was on top of the fact that I'd been married for only four months—there might have been a few minor adjustments I needed to make so I could be a good husband. But that's not all. My parents were going through a rough time in their marriage. Like a normal guy, I compartmentalized all of these stresses to keep everything under control.

Finally, it all blew up. Minutes before I was to lead a worship rehearsal for a Sunday evening service, I received an urgent telephone call from my Mom and Dad. They had my sister and I on a three-way call from Houston. As gently as they could, they broke the news that after 29 years of marriage, they were getting a divorce.

I was stunned. I felt crushed. I knew they were struggling, but I'd never dreamed things would come to this point. I hung up the phone and walked back into the worship rehearsal. I tried to act like nothing had happened, but all of the stress I'd fought back for months felt like a volcano erupting inside me. I looked at the worship team, but I was mute. I realized I couldn't continue. I asked them to give me a minute. I walked off-stage and into Pastor Wilson's office. As I opened the door, he was sitting at his desk. I slowly closed the door, turned around, opened my mouth to explain what had happened, and began to sob like a baby. At that time in my life, I wasn't used to crying because I'd repressed every painful emotion for a long time. It was a big deal to experience honest emotions and let them out in tears, but this was no ordinary cry. My sobs released months of tension from a body and mind that was stressed to the breaking point. Pastor Wilson prayed with me. He walked with me out to my car and sent me home to be with Cherith. I cried for hours. I'm afraid it scared Cherith half to death.

What in the world was going on with me? I'd never had a reaction like this in my life. I'd always handled difficult times calmly and had never lost control. Why did this news cause such a strong reaction? Actually, it had nothing to do with the news of my parents' divorce. It had everything to do with the fact that I'd reached the breaking point after years of trying to do way too much ministry on my own. The explosion of emotions was the result of years of over-responsibility, poor delegation, and hyper-control. For years, I'd been wearing myself too thin. I was so determined to be "the man" and to be "in charge" that I never delegated any authority to anyone in our Kids Ministry. I was determined to do it all myself. Oh, I had some very competent volunteers over the years, but they never stuck with me very long because they never felt needed or valued. They were high caliber people, but I did everything while they were forced to sit and watch.

My cataclysmic meltdown occurred because I was determined to do all the work of the ministry on my own. The call from my parents was "the straw that broke the camel's back." It was a huge mistake in my ministry—one that almost cost me my sanity.

My mistake: Trying to be the Lone Ranger
instead of building a team.

I have a sneaking suspicion that I'm not the only one riding this horse. People in every walk of life and ministers in every role in churches can conclude that they have to do it all. When they begin a new role, they're excited about their vision and the opportunities. At first, they want to have their hands in everything. One of the most important tasks of a good leader, though, is to recruit, equip, and train competent, qualified, eager people to come along and help. There are many reasons we may fail to do this essential task of leadership. They all seem perfectly rational, but they result in disaster. Being a Lone Ranger may make a good television show, but it makes a lousy leader.

Why Do We Go It Alone?

As I've looked at my own life and talked to hundreds of kids' ministry leaders across the country, I've noticed several reasons we hold too tightly to control and fail to delegate. Here are the most common ones I've found:

We think we're too busy to recruit and equip a team.

This reason is number one on the list. I can't tell you how many times an overworked kids' ministry leader has complained, "Recruiting a team takes so much work. I don't have time for all of that. I'm too busy doing the work of the ministry to stop and ask people to join me. And if they agreed, I'd have to spend tons of time training them. That's time I just don't have. It's a lot easier just to do it myself."

These people don't realize just how ludicrous their excuses sound. It reminds me of the story of two men who were assigned to move two piles of bricks from one side of the brickyard to the other. Both piles were exactly the same size: 5,000 bricks. The first man started carrying his bricks and found he could carry about ten bricks at a time. He looked over at the other man and noticed he was walking away. "Hey! Where are you going?" he yelled.

The other man yelled back, "I'm going to get some help!"

The first man thought the other guy was foolish. He wondered, *Why in the world is he wasting his time trying to go find someone to help him? In the amount of time he spends trying to find help, he could move 1,000 bricks. He's crazy!*

Twenty minutes later, the second man came back with five friends. All six of them carried bricks while the first man still slugged it out by himself. In very little time, the second man's pile of bricks was completely moved while the first man stared at the huge pile he still needed to carry away.

Which man was foolish? The second man spent valuable time off the job recruiting helpers, but his efforts paid off. The first man was fiercely determined and never quit, but he wasn't smart. By the time he was finished, he was exhausted, and it took him far longer than the six men required to move the other pile of bricks.

If this is your excuse, stop telling yourself that you're too busy to build a team. Yes, it takes time and effort, but the rewards are worth it.

We feel like second-class leaders in the church.

Self-pity is not a desirable leadership trait—in any industry, profession, or ministry. I've heard many kids' pastors complain, "Nobody wants to help me, so I have to do it on my own." They moan and whine about the lack of help they receive. When I press them to explain, they often admit they haven't even asked anyone. They just assumed that since there aren't scores of people lining up in the hallway to volunteer to help, no one is willing to serve. Kids' ministries don't get a lot of "face time" in some churches, so the leaders don't feel valued. They need to get their vision and calling from the Lord and serve Him gladly. They aren't second-class in His eyes!

We're afraid to ask.

Many people in ministry are Lone Rangers because they're afraid to ask people to join the team. It takes guts to ask someone to step up and be a part of the ministry team. They might say "no," they might ask hard questions, or they might require more attention than we want to give. We need wisdom to know who to ask and how to ask them, but we don't need to be afraid to ask people to become part of a life-changing ministry. Serving in kids' ministries is God's divine work, and it's one of the greatest privileges in our lives. Ask boldly. This is kingdom stuff.

I believe there are people in every church who are waiting for us to ask them to join us. If we wait until they volunteer, we may be waiting a long time. Merely placing a blurb in the Sunday morning bulletin doesn't work any more. People want to be personally invited to invest their time and talents. Don't assume people are reluctant. Most people are eager to help, but they want someone to ask them to be involved. They want to use their gifts and talents, and they want to feel needed. They're just waiting on you to ask them, so man up and ask them!

Our egos get in the way.

Let's be painfully honest: One of the main reasons kids' ministry leaders insist on doing it all themselves is that their egos won't let them share the spotlight. They enjoy the thrill of being on stage. They get an adrenaline rush from being "the man" or "the woman" who's indispensable.

This can't be you, can it? Maybe not. I would have denied it before my meltdown, but it was absolutely true for me. Take an honest inventory of your heart and motives. Ask hard questions, and let God's Spirit reveal your hidden desires. Is your ego keeping you from building a team?

We're convinced nobody can do it as well as we can.

Excellence is important, but we make a strategic mistake when we conclude that we're the only ones who can do things the way they really need to be done. And we may have forgotten that we made plenty of mistakes when we started. Someone let us go through the learning curve so we could gain insights and skills. Maybe we need to be as gracious to the people around us.

A big part of excellence in leadership is being devoted to the process of building a great team. If we insist on doing everything ourselves, we devalue the people who are dedicated to our mission. That's dumb, and it's destructive. We'll never have people on our team who can do it as well as we can unless we let them try!

We think, **It's faster if I just do it myself.**

This assumption is true if there's a very limited vision with a very limited set of activities. After all, I prefer to brush my teeth myself instead of delegating it to my kids! But as a ministry grows and becomes more complex, we'll stunt the growth if we insist on doing it all on our own. Certainly, it takes time to train people to do a job effectively. When we train people and duplicate ourselves, however, far more will be accomplished and more lives will be changed. We need to look at the long-term benefits of investing some time in equipping people to serve effectively.

The Benefits of Building a Team

I had to learn the hard way, but I discovered life is far better when I have a great team around me. I experience benefits in many different ways:

Teams are a lot more fun.

When I tried to be a Lone Ranger, I felt stressed, and the people around me didn't feel valued. They were eager to help, but my insistence on being totally in control created confusion. As I began to equip them and trust them, they thrived. And we have a blast together! (Why did it take me so long?) One of the core values of First

One of the core values of First Assembly NLR states, "Everything is better in teams." I see this lived out every day in our Kids Ministry.

Assembly NLR states, "Everything is better in teams." I see this lived out every day in our Kids Ministry.

Teams help us avoid burnout.

Countless leaders have experienced meltdowns like mine. All of us have limits. If we don't learn to resolve stress, the cumulative effect will eventually take its toll. We have different points of vulnerability, but we all have one. Excess, unrelieved stress may show up in headaches, stomach problems, or relational tension. Some of us become driven and demanding; some become depressed. No matter how talented we may be, and no matter how clearly God has called us, we won't last if we insist on doing all the work. Burnout isn't a mild condition that is easily remedied. It takes months or even years to recover.

Teams make room for growth.

If we insist on being a Lone Ranger and refuse to build a team, our foolish choice will limit the potential of our ministry. Even those who are the most talented and driven can only accomplish a finite amount of work on their own. The size and effectiveness of a ministry doesn't depend on one person. It depends on the number of committed, passionate, effective leaders we involve. We'll accomplish far more for God and His kingdom if we learn to recruit, train, and delegate to the wonderful people who want to join us in kids' ministry. When we insist on being the center of attention and a Lone Ranger, we have decided that stroking our egos is more important than reaching as many children as possible for the kingdom. I don't want to stand before God and tell Him, "I would have done more, but I didn't want to share the spotlight."

Teams allow others to use their God-given gifts and talents.

Men and women who have been gifted and called by God to join us in working with kids are all around us. When we demand to do it all ourselves, we deprive them of the joy of fulfilling their God-given potential.

Teams prepare the ministry for the future.

We may not be able to imagine ever doing anything other than working with the kids and volunteers in our present situation, but sooner or later, most of us will move on to something else. If we build a strong team, one of the members may rise up to replace us when we leave, or the team will provide a stable environment for a new person who comes as the new kids' pastor. Without a great team, kids' ministries can implode when the leader leaves. (Or they may rejoice, which is really sad.) When we build a team, pour into the members, and multiply ourselves, we prepare the ministry for the future.

Teams help us minister to all kinds of kids.

Some kids connect with you and your personality, but some don't. A team that consists of people from various backgrounds and with different personalities allows your ministry to connect with a wide array of kids.

A Few Examples from the Scriptures

Teams have always been central to God's plan to reach the lost and build disciples. Equipping and delegating aren't secondary to the Great Commission; they're an important part of it. From David's mighty men to the missionary teams in Acts, God has used teams to accomplish His purposes.

Moses had a Lone Ranger mentality, and he suffered for it. He led the people out of Egypt into the Wilderness. He believed he was the only one responsible to handle the civil, criminal, and family disputes of two million people! (And you thought you had it bad.) He was on the verge of burnout when his father-in-law, Jethro, confronted him and told him to appoint 70 men to help him lead the people. Moses listened and picked the men. I'm not sure if he was wise enough or desperate enough, but he took Jethro's advice (see Exodus 18:13f).

When David was running away from Saul, God gave him some friends who believed in him, supported him, and defended him with their lives. David must have been a great leader because he attracted the very best men in the land to join him in a seemingly hopeless cause. Together, they trusted God and fought like crazy—and they won (see 1 Chronicles 11).

When Nehemiah planned to rebuild the walls of Jerusalem after the nation had been devastated by other nations, he devised a shrewd plan. He enlisted all the people to help in the work, and he asked them to build the part of the wall near their homes. They were highly motivated to protect their families, and they completed the task in an incredibly short time.

Paul was one of the bravest, most daring men of all time, but he seldom did any work for God without a trusted partner. Barnabas, Silas, Timothy, and others joined him in taking the gospel to the Roman world. Paul was fiercely dedicated, but he knew the value of having a partner with him all the time.

Even Jesus, the matchless Son of God, the creator of all that exists, wasn't a Lone Ranger. He assembled a team of twelve men to be His chosen disciples, but in many accounts, we find a larger entourage of men and women who followed Him wherever He went. To these people, Jesus entrusted the Great Commission, the most sweeping, grand, and glorious enterprise the world has ever known. Today, about two billion people claim to be His followers. We are part of the legacy of those first followers, and we're now part of His team.

Each of us should strive to do the work of the ministry with a gifted, passionate, dedicated team of believers. I used to be a Lone Ranger, but no longer. Now, I never do ministry alone. When I make a home visit, I bring someone along. When I'm speaking at a conference, I take someone with me. When I'm visiting a child in the hospital, I try to take someone on our team or a person who might join our team. I want to take every opportunity to add to the ministry team God has called me to lead.

> Each of us should strive to do the work of the ministry with a gifted, passionate, dedicated team of believers. I used to be a Lone Ranger, but no longer. Now, I never do ministry alone.

Children are amazing. The opportunity to minister to children is one of the highest honors and deepest pleasures in life. It's also one of the most challenging. We're selfish and foolish if we try to do it alone. And we forget that even the Lone Ranger had Tonto.

Recruiting a Volunteer Team

I can hear someone say, "Okay, Brian, you've convinced me! I'm ready to recruit and build a team, but I don't know how. I've tried, but it didn't work. Can you help me?"

I'm certainly not an expert in recruiting. I have had my own struggles in building a volunteer team, but failure can be a terrific teacher. There's no magic formula. The only way to recruit successfully is continuous hard work and tenacity to apply a few key principles. I want to share some of the insights and practices that have guided me:

Never recruit for a need. Instead, recruit for an opportunity.

There is nothing less attractive than a Children's Ministry Director standing up in front of the congregation and saying, "We're swamped. We're overwhelmed. We have to have some help! Will you please help us before we collapse?"

What do you think the person listening actually hears in this plea? It screams, "There's a really good reason no one is working with them!"

Here's a free pointer: Never use the phrase, "No one wants to help us" or "I can't get anyone to help me." People's natural, instinctive (and wise) reaction to these statements is to avoid working with you. When you begin a recruitment pitch with negative words, it's like my son, Jordan, beginning a request by saying, "Dad, I know you're going to say 'No,' but . . ." My immediate response is always "No!" And he's given me permission to give that answer. In fact, I can answer before he finishes the question. I'm trying to train him not to talk me out of agreeing with him before he asks the question. And I'm trying to train kids' ministry leaders in the same way.

Rather than moan about being desperate for help, celebrate the growth and excitement of your kids' ministry. Don't talk about what you don't have, talk about what you have—opportunities for the volunteers of your church to work on a great team and make an eternal impact in the lives of kids.

Share the vision of your ministry.

A clear, compelling vision of changed lives captures the hearts of those who might volunteer to join your team. Share stories in church services about God working to change the lives of kids and their families. Also, ask team members to share stories about how God has touched them as they've served in the ministry. Being a volunteer in children's ministry is an incredible opportunity to honor God—not a rigid duty or an empty task.

When you're recruiting prospective team members, you can tell them, "God is going to accomplish His plan in the lives of the children in our church. The question isn't 'Will God do it?' The question is 'Do you want to be a part of it?'"

Recruit one-on-one and face-to-face.

Rather than putting a global, impersonal request in the bulletin, producing a video segment, or begging for a pulpit spot from your senior pastor, recruit by approaching people one-on-one and having a meaningful conversation with them.

Ask God to show you the people He's preparing to join you. When He puts someone on your heart, make an appointment so you have time to share your vision and answer questions. Don't just walk up in the hallway at church and give a quick invitation. That doesn't communicate value or respect—or good planning. Instead, invite the person to lunch or, at least, talk on the phone

Rather than putting a global, impersonal request in the bulletin, producing a video segment, or begging for a pulpit spot from your senior pastor, recruit by approaching people one-on-one and having a meaningful conversation with them.

when you and the person aren't rushed or distracted. Explain, "I wanted to talk to you because I believe God has given you a heart for kids and the skills to make a difference in their lives." Most people will have plenty of questions. Remember: There are no stupid questions! Some people will give you an immediate response, but others will want time to think and pray about it. Respect the process for each person.

Recruit volunteers based on their gifts.

Don't recruit a volunteer simply to complete a task. In other words, don't say, "I need someone to take care of my fifth grade boys' class." Take time to uncover the person's desires and spiritual gifts. If they're not sure about their gifts, you can use an online inventory[1] or one your church uses for other ministries. Find a role that best fits the person's gifts, talents, and interests. For example, don't stick a person who is gifted in teaching in the corner taking attendance. Honor every person's heart and God-given abilities.

Develop a ministry application for volunteers to complete.

If you don't already have one, create an application that gathers important contact information and asks pertinent questions to provide insight into the person. What are their likes and dislikes? What experience do they have working with kids? What are their gifts and talents? What do they consider "success" in ministry?

Always include a criminal background check and personal references. Virtually every church leader can cite painful incidences when adults harmed children. Conduct due diligence to minimize the risk. It's your responsibility to make sure kids are protected when they come to learn about God.

A standardized, comprehensive application elevates the importance of the ministry in the applicant's eyes—and in the eyes of parents. It tells everyone about your dedication to create a safe and secure environment. [2]

Ask for feedback and input from other staff pastors and your senior pastor before finalizing a person's position on your team.

The staff of your church can be an excellent source to screen people who might become volunteers in your kids' ministry. They may be aware of situations in the applicant's life that precludes him or her from being involved in ministry—at least at the present time. This may involve spiritual problems, emotional difficulties, or family disputes. Also, the person may be serving in other areas of ministry and may already be stretched too thin.

It would be wise to get input from your pastor even *before* you approach the person about getting involved. Ask for a few minutes in a staff meeting or privately with your pastor to ask for input. A little caution will help you immensely and save you a world of hurt!

Develop a job description and clearly communicate your expectations.

Don't expect volunteers to "just know" what they need to do. For every responsibility, develop a job description to avoid confusion. Muddy expectations inevitably lead to confusion, disappointment, and conflict. It takes some time to craft clear, workable job descriptions, but once you have them, they're invaluable. You can create your own or adapt those used at another church.[3]

Partner the new recruit with an effective member of your team.

The best way for someone to learn how to do a job effectively is to watch someone else in action. Find the member of your team who is really knocking it out of the park and connect the new recruit with that person for at least three weeks. Allow the new recruit to observe not only what the veteran does, but also what she doesn't do. Leave the door open for the new recruit to come back and ask questions to clarify roles and responsibilities.

Encourage your entire volunteer team to be relentless recruiters.

You shouldn't be the only one pumping up the ministry and asking others to be involved. People expect you to recruit volunteers, but in truth, the best recruiters are the volunteers who connect so closely with kids and parents. People may feel they can blow me off when I ask them to join our team, but they highly respect other volunteers who are their peers and who love being involved in our ministry.

Leading a time of prayer with several members of our team.

Look for FAT CATS

You need to make sure you choose the right kind of people to be your team members. It's not about just "getting a warm body" to sit in this classroom with these kids. Look for people who will be part of a terrific team. You want a bunch of FAT CATS!

F – Faithful

When I think of people who are faithful, I think of Donnie Miller, who has been on our Kids Ministry team for the last eight years. He's a dad who has volunteered to serve as our Security Team Director. I know I can always count on him. If he says he'll be there at 5:00, he's there at 4:55. He travels a lot for his job, but Donnie always emails me his schedule. He understands the importance of his ministry position and has a track record of faithfulness. I thank God for people like Donnie. I want our entire ministry team to mirror his faithfulness.

When you assemble your ministry team, look for those who are faithful. In a parable about a faithful steward, the master told him, "Well done, good and faithful servant! You have been faithful with a few things; I will put you in charge of many things" (Matthew 25:19). That's what I want to hear from God, and I'm looking for volunteers with the same heart and commitment.

A – Available

Being available isn't about "not having anything else to do." It's is an attitude that says, "I'm willing to serve in any capacity that advances the kingdom of God."

When I think of available, I think of Jason Fleming, a professional in the medical field. His schedule is crazy, and he works a nonsensical amount of hours, but Jason is always willing to serve in whatever capacity I ask. He has served as the Sunday School Director, the Kids Choir Director, a nursery worker, a substitute teacher and even more roles.

When you're assembling your team, recruit people like Jason, people who are available to serve wherever they're needed because they have a passion to reach kids. I'm wary of people who have an "I don't do windows" mentality. You want people like Isaiah, who told God, "Here am I. Send me!" (Isaiah 6:8)

T – Teachable

I've been in kids' ministry for twenty years, and I still have a lot to learn. To be effective and to work well on a team, a person must be open and teachable. And besides, the more you learn, the more you find out just how much you still don't know.

One of the most teachable members of our team is Fred Dickson. He's been the director of our Junior Bible Quiz team for 33 years. (That's as long as Jesus was alive on earth. Fred loves it when I point that out.) He's the head of the tech department at a national insurance company and has enormous executive and ministry experience. If anyone has a reason to sit back, put it in park, and no longer grow, it's Fred. But he continuously asks me for advice and feedback about his plans for his area of ministry. He understands that a ministry team grows only as much as its leader is willing to grow.

C – Committed

In our society, commitment is a quality that seems to be waning. Whether it is commitment to a career, a marriage, or a church, many people believe they can bail out at the slightest inconvenience. Being committed means a person will "stick with it" no matter how difficult the conditions. On our team, that's Katheryn Whitener, one of the most talented teachers I've ever seen. The kids love her. As a result, her class grows . . . sometimes too much, too quickly. Recently, she had twice the number of students that other classes had. Her supplies were low and her energy was being drained, but Katheryn pressed on to teach her class with joy and creativity. With a smile on her face, she's committed to the God-given privilege of teaching kids.

A – Accountable

Accountability is something we often want from others, but we rarely want to give. On a ministry team, accountability is crucial for things to run smoothly. When you're building your ministry team, be very cautious about those who have a reputation of refusing to submit to authority. Value those who are willing to be accountable to you as their spiritual leader.

George Weaver has been on the Children's Ministry team in our church since before I arrived twelve years ago. He's now the director of our weekly ministry to boys, called Royal Rangers, which is a mentoring program in the Assemblies of God that teaches camping and life skills to boys. When other kids' pastors groan when they talk about the Royal Rangers' leaders at their church, I can't relate. I beam when I talk about George. He's learned that accountability should be offered, not demanded. He consistently sends me emails and text messages or calls to give me information about his area of ministry. When he's not able to make it, he doesn't wait for me to ask, "Where were you?" Instead, he voluntarily informs me far in advance when he will be gone.

When George makes a mistake, he owns up to it. I remember several years ago when, in the heat of the moment, he handled a situation in the wrong way. When he realized it, he didn't try to make excuses for what he had done or argue that his way was right. Instead, he called and explained what he had done wrong and asked for advice on how to make it right. He's the kind of person who makes serving on a ministry team so rewarding.

T – Transparent

Too often, we wear masks to hide our feelings and our character. We don't want to admit our faults, our weaknesses, or our failures. On a ministry team, this works against our efforts to become a team with authentic relationships. When you can't share your feelings, fears, or failures with someone, trust ceases to exist. Without trust, every team becomes distant and disjointed. When we project a false version of ourselves for others to see, we're pretentious and fake. Rather than be transparent, we put up walls between us and other team members.

Josh Clinton was a typical twenty-three-year-old. He attended college, hung out with friends, and enjoyed life. But one thing about Josh isn't typical. He's one of the most transparent young men I've ever met. To know Josh is to know his heart, his passions, his strengths, and his weaknesses. He doesn't try to be something he isn't. He allows his God-given abilities and weaknesses to be seen by every member of our Kids Ministry team. I appreciate his honesty, so I hired him on our full-time staff.

Transparency is a basic requirement for each member of your ministry team. Actually, transparency is about integrity, and it's essential if a team wants to enjoy rich, real, and powerful relationships. It builds trust and breaks down walls. Paul wrote, "Let our lives lovingly express the truth (in all things speaking truly, dealing truly, living truly)" (Ephesians 4:15 Amplified Bible).

S – Serving

The great Chicago preacher, Dwight L. Moody, once said, "The measure of a man is not how many servants he has, but how many men he serves." One of the most important traits of anyone in ministry is having a heart for serving others.

What is ministry all about? It's about serving others. As we minister to children, we'll be required to do things that are out of our comfort zone (such as playing crazy characters, getting hit in the face with pies, and going to lock-ins, just to name a few). We need a heart that says, "Whatever I have to do to reach these kids, I'll do it!"

Victor Rodriguez has a true servant's heart. He's a third-degree black belt who works for the Police Department. If there's anyone who could easily impose himself on others, it's Victor. But he displays a tender, serving heart to the children in our church. It's not uncommon to walk into the room to find Victor sitting on the floor talking to a child or running around the room with two or three boys hanging on his back. He loves to serve kids.

Victor also serves his leaders. I've received many phone calls and emails from him, asking what he can do to serve me. He wants to do what he can to make my job easier. Jesus said, "Anyone who wants to be the first must take last place and be the servant of everyone else" (Mark 9:35). Victor lives this commitment every day.

At the end of every major event in our ministry, the volunteers faithfully stay until the last chair is put away and the last piece of trash is thrown away. Before they leave, I ask them to gather around, and I tell them, "God has used you in a huge way today. I appreciate you so much. These kids and their families are different because God has used you to pour Himself into them. Thank you so much for being part of this team!" I give them all fist bumps, and we have a cheer like a football team that just won a big game. That's exactly the way we feel—because we're a winning team. I make a note of who's there at the end, and I send them personal notes to thank them. If I were still a Lone Ranger, we'd all miss out on these wonderful moments.

In our communities, we have countless children to reach and little time to reach them. We need to partner with those who are faithful, available, teachable, committed, accountable, and transparent, and those who are serving in order to accomplish the Great Commission. As you build your team, remember this: Never settle! It's better to have an unfilled position than the wrong person on your team. After someone has been recruited and placed in a role, it's very difficult to "un-recruit" him. Pray, think, and strategize. Ask God to give you a terrific team. As you talk to people, share your heart and your vision and begin building your team for the future. It's time to stop making the mistake of being a Lone Ranger in ministry and get some FAT CATS on your kids' ministry team!

> As you build your team, remember this: Never settle! It's better to have an unfilled position than the wrong person on your team.

Think about it...

1. What are some excuses you've heard (or said) for a kids' ministry leader being a Lone Ranger?

2. Which of the benefits of a team seem most attractive to you? Explain your answer.

3. What are your strengths in recruiting a great team? What principles do you need to sharpen? What difference will it make to improve in those areas?

4. As you look at your existing team, who are the FAT CATS? Who are the ones who can become FAT CATS with a little time, attention, and training? Is there anyone who just doesn't fit and isn't open to your input?

5. What's the one thing you need to focus on to build a better team?

"Who cares about 'big church'?" 7

I was really ticked.

One Monday in a staff meeting, Pastor Rod gave a glowing report about how God had worked the day before in our worship services. All the other staff members were on the edge of their seats, waiting for a grand announcement, but I had no clue what they were waiting on. It was like walking in at the middle of a movie. Slowly, I began to put the pieces together. He explained (in a way that assumed everybody already knew exactly what he was talking about) that our people had given over $90,000 to translate the Bible into the Farsi language. He beamed, "It's the biggest single day offering in our church's history!"

They celebrated. I boiled. How could it happen that every person on earth (or at least in the staff meeting) except me was well aware of this ministry and the offering? When had it been announced? Who had talked about it? Why didn't somebody tell me what was going on? I felt angry, overlooked, and taken for granted. I'd been working like crazy to build the very best Kids Ministry at our church, but I was seldom in the main worship services.

After the staff meeting, I talked to Pastor Rod, "I'm not sure what's going on. Why didn't somebody tell me about this offering before it was taken? I would have loved to have been a part of it."

He could tell I was mad, but his reply was unflappable. He said, "Brian, I'm not sure why you didn't know about it. We've talked about it on Sundays for the past month or so."

Instantly, I barked, "Well, I'm not in there on Sundays, so how could I ever know about things like this? It's a little unfair that those of us who aren't able to attend the service on Sunday morning are in the dark about things like this. It's not our fault."

Pastor Rod, in his ever-patient way, asked me a series of questions. He said, "I see. We had a giant announcement in the bulletin for the past several weeks. Didn't you read the bulletin?"

I had to answer, "No, I didn't have time to read it."

He continued, "I sent a long letter out to the entire church, explaining the opportunity to provide Bibles in the Farsi language. Did you read that?"

I sadly had to answer, "No, I saw the letter on the counter at home, but I didn't read it."

He replied, "We've talked about it in the past several staff meetings. Don't you remember those?"

By now, my voice barely registered in the audible range. "No, I don't remember. Maybe, I wasn't paying attention."

That ended our conversation. My anger morphed into embarrassment. The irony, of course, is that I'd been furious about feeling left out when I'd chosen to ignore all the communication. I assumed, "If it doesn't have anything to do with Kids Ministry, I don't really

> Every children's ministry pastor and volunteer has to overcome the obstacle of being isolated to some degree from the mainstream of church life.

need to pay attention to it." I'd made a very big mistake that many Kids Ministry leaders make.

My mistake: Having tunnel vision and missing the big picture.

Every children's ministry pastor and volunteer has to overcome the obstacle of being isolated to some degree from the mainstream of church life. We're passionate about kids and excited about our roles, but it's easy for us to develop a "silo mentality." A silo occurs when each part of an organization becomes self-contained, is independent from the others, and fails to coordinate vision, philosophy, and practices. It can happen in divisions of companies, and it can happen in churches—especially in kids' ministries.

In the months (and probably years) before the conversation with Pastor Rod after the staff meeting, I'd become radically devoted to our ministry to children. There was nothing wrong with that, but before I realized it, I saw our ministry as a silo. I didn't do anything to resolve it. I didn't take the initiative to find out more about the mainstream of what our church was doing. And in fact, I didn't even take a few minutes to read newsletters or pay attention in staff meetings. I didn't even care what "they" were doing because I was so committed to what "we" were doing. I was building my own little kingdom, and I resented anyone who didn't contribute to our success. I only paid attention to other pastors and church leaders if their input applied directly to Kids Ministry.

The Dangers of Tunnel Vision

The leadership term "tunnel vision" is borrowed from the physical condition, which occurs when an individual loses peripheral vision (the ability to see objects on the top, bottom, and sides). The result is a very constricted field of vision. In organizations, a manager with tunnel vision is zoned-in on his single priority, and he doesn't see much else. Being focused is good and helpful, but not in the extreme.

In kids' ministries, we need to recognize the symptoms of tunnel vision. If we don't, we may suffer severe consequences. Here are some dangers for kids' pastors and other leaders:

We develop a territorial spirit.

When we're operating in a silo, we develop an "us against them" mentality. We think, *I do Kids Ministry. Let them worry about the adult ministry stuff. Besides, we're doing what really counts.* This attitude is poisonous and causes division in the church.

> It's exhilarating to have a deep sense that God has equipped us for a particular role in ministry. But the sheer joy of serving God can drift into arrogance and ruin the individual and everything he touches.

It's a wonderful thing to believe that what we do really matters. It's terrific to see God work to change lives. It's exhilarating to have a deep sense that God has equipped us for a particular role in ministry. But the sheer joy of serving God can drift into arrogance and ruin the individual and everything he touches.

When I was at The Oaks, I received a call on a Saturday from Scott Wilson, who, at the time, was the Youth Pastor/Associate Pastor. The bass player for the regular worship service was sick, so he asked if he could use my bass player from my Young Warriors (the fourth-to sixth-grade service). I had some special music planned for my service, and I was angry that he would even ask! In fact, I even threatened to quit my job. I snarled, "Obviously, no one cares enough about Kids Ministry. We always get the leftovers!"

I failed to grasp that Sunday morning worship is central to the calling and strategy of the church. I've heard many times, "Sunday morning in the sanctuary pays the bills. If it's not excellent, everything suffers." But for some reason, I gradually began to see every other ministry and event as competition to our Kids Ministry. When Scott called, he wasn't demanding or rude. He simply made a request. I'd become so fiercely territorial that I felt he was trying to take "my" bass player away.

We develop a "poor me" mentality.

When we don't feel appreciated, it's not a big step from being territorial to being consumed with self-pity. When we feel like second-class ministers, we feel persecuted, and every perceived slight hurts like the blow from an ax! In fact, one of the signs that we've crossed the line is when we become overly upset over a perceived injustice. A healthy person would ask questions to clarify things, but a fragile, furious person takes offense even when no offense has occurred.

We infect the rest of our team.

In our ministry, I was the model, the example, and the one who others looked to for leadership. What did they see? I had become a person who often complained, "Everyone else gets to be in the sanctuary while we're *slaving away* ministering to kids!" Others copied my attitude and words. I'd created a culture of resentment. It wasn't pretty.

A workhorse may be more effective if it wears blinders, but blinders are lethal in organizations. Kids' ministry leaders with tunnel vision can be so narrowly focused that they become cut off from the rest of the church. A sense of isolation on the kids' ministry team leads to more complaints than praise, eventually decreasing effectiveness of the ministry and the church.

We fail to support (and may even compete with) the pastor's vision.

You can't communicate what you don't understand. If you aren't connected with the pastor's vision, you end up casting your own vision—which may be different from his. Remember, the only reason you have your job is because your pastor can't be everywhere at the same time. God has called your pastor to lead the church. Your task is to support him and his vision for the church, the community, and the future.

We fail to communicate key information to parents and team members.

I'm lucky no one asked me any questions about the Farsi Bible offering, or I would have looked completely stupid. When we create silos, we don't value information about other areas of ministry—or the church itself. If a parent or kids' ministry team member needs some information about an event, we're clueless. In fact, we may gently (or not so gently) ridicule the person for even asking about an event that's not central to kids' ministry. Sadly, some parents and other adults don't even ask the Kids Pastor about events pertaining to the church because he has a reputation for "only caring about his area."

We make it difficult for kids and team members to transition to other ministries.

In organizations with silos, leaders demand complete, unquestioned loyalty from team members and unbridled enthusiasm from participants. Too often, I've seen insecure kids' ministers subtly (or not so subtly) disparage their pastor and other ministries in the church. They hope to win loyalty among their people by putting others down. When their people interact with others in the church, or when they move into other roles, they carry their "us against them" attitude with them.

In many churches, a rivalry exists between the children's ministry and the youth ministry. Competition can be fierce. They're both serving God, and they are both part of the same vision, but they draw on the same pool of potential volunteers, and their schedules can conflict. And there's one more potential problem: The leaders of both ministries may be young—not tempered and flexible enough to gracefully and wisely handle points of conflict.

We miss the joy of being involved in something bigger than ourselves.

When we build ourselves up by putting others down, we get an adrenaline rush every time we feel disregarded. Resentment gives us two things we value: identity and energy. We believe we're "the one who was wronged," so we feel justified in our anger. And seeing ourselves as the offended party gives us a surge of energy. It's addictive! But it's incredibly dangerous because it's against everything Jesus died for: love, humility, patience, joy, and sacrifice. But there's another price we pay when we create silos: We miss the joy of celebrating God's magnificent work throughout the church, in every ministry, and in every person's life.

Two Examples

There are plenty of painful examples of leaders with tunnel vision, but I want to highlight two. Before leading God's people into the Promised Land, Moses sent twelve spies to scope out the land and the people who lived there. When they returned, they gave two very different stories: the

majority report and the minority report.

But there's another price we pay when we create silos: We miss the joy of celebrating God's magnificent work throughout the church, in every ministry, and in every person's life.

Ten of the spies said the land was abundant with milk, honey, fruit, and every other good thing. However, when they saw the strength of the people who lived in Canaan, they were terrified, and their vision narrowed to a dot. God's power had just been on display in the ten plagues and parting the Red Sea, and God had promised to give them strength to conquer the land. But they couldn't see any of that. All they saw were the problems they'd face if they trusted God and marched into the land. In contrast, Joshua and Caleb delivered the minority report. (By the way, can you name any of the ten doubters? I didn't think so. The memory of those with tunnel vision has faded from our collective memories.) These two men saw the difficulties, but they had a far bigger, wider, more expansive vision of God's power to accomplish His promises (Numbers 13:1-33). The people, though, sided with the ten. They spent forty long years in the desert until everyone but Joshua and Caleb had died. These two men led the children of Israel into the land God had promised them.

When Rome invaded Palestine and conquered it, the new governors wanted to introduce Roman and Greek culture into this part of the Empire. To remain faithful to the Scriptures and their traditions, the Jewish leaders, the Pharisees, defended their laws at all costs. Their vision of God's purposes, however, wasn't big enough to include the possibility of a person who would turn everything upside down. When Jesus healed on the Sabbath, the Pharisees were outraged! In fact, from early in Jesus' ministry, they plotted to have Him killed (Mark 3:1-6). Talk about missing the forest for the trees! They hated Him and conspired to kill the Son of God because they were so narrow and rigid in defending the letter of God's law!

Tunnel vision isn't just an inconvenience. It's an acid that eats away at everything good, right, noble, and pure in a leader's heart, a team's life, and a ministry's impact.

Avoiding Tunnel Vision

It's not enough to sit back and expect your pastor or other staff members to make sure you're vitally connected with the entire scope of the church's life. That's your responsibility. Here are some steps you can take to stay in touch:

Read every available piece of information.

Make it a weekly practice to read the bulletin, newsletters, articles on the website, and anything else that tells what the church is doing. Most churches do a good job of getting information out to their people, including the staff, but it's up to each of us to take a few minutes to read it—and that's all it takes, just a few minutes.

Ask questions.

If you're unsure about an upcoming event, a strategy, or any other plan, take the initiative to get answers to your questions. In fact, I'm so dense that

I often ask, "Is there anything going on that I haven't asked about?" Don't wait for others to spoon feed you adequate information. In staff meetings, ask your pastor and other staff members if they have any information they want you to communicate to your volunteers, parents, or kids.

Watch or listen to the Sunday morning service.

Most churches record the pastor's sermon each week. If you can't attend the service (and you can't), make it a priority to listen to the message sometime during the week. It will keep you connected to the pastor and to the heartbeat of the church.

At lunch every Sunday at our church, I play a DVD of the morning service while our Kids Ministry team has lunch together. We enjoy hanging out with each other, everybody likes to eat, and we stay connected to what happened in our church that morning. Also, it sends a loud, clear message to our team that I want them to be exposed to Pastor Rod's vision every week.

Pay attention in staff meetings.

Maybe, this one is just for me. After my talk with Pastor Rod, I realized I hadn't given my undivided attention in staff meetings. I had to make a change. When other pastors had been sharing what was going on in their ministry areas, I'd been checking email, updating my website, and daydreaming. I was sure none of what was going on in the meeting affected me at all, so I tuned out. But I'd missed important information, felt disconnected, and made wrong assumptions about everyone in the room.

Regularly pray for your pastor and other department leaders.

In my relationships with other pastors at our church, I want to go beyond collecting raw information and coordinating schedules. I've made a
heartfelt commitment to each person on our pastoral team. I make a point
to ask them questions about what's going on in their personal lives and ministries, and (get this) I'm committed to really listen when they tell me what's
going on. In addition, I pray for them. I ask for specific prayer requests, and I
check up on them to see how God has worked. This choice has made a huge
difference in my perspective, my attitude, and my relationships with each
person on the team. They've told me the greatest challenges they face in
their ministries, and I've found out their joys and struggles in their families.
My commitment to pray for them has kept me connected and prevented me
from becoming focused only on Kids Ministry.

Communicate the pastor's heart and vision.

We've come a long way since I realized I'd created a silo with barbed
wire and concrete walls. Now, I work with my pastor so we communicate
the same message with the same heart. We want the DNA of the church to
reach into every corner of every home. One of Pastor Rod's most famous
statements is "Every soul matters to God." He teaches that the most obscure
person in a forgotten land is as valuable to God as the soul of a celebrity. I
teach it to the kids, too. When our Junior Bible Quiz team came up with a
name, they didn't call themselves the Panthers, Cardinals, Jaguars, or Ra-
zorbacks. They chose ESMTG: Every Soul Matters to God. That's a good
sign that the pastor's heart has filtered down through me into the children's
hearts. Our kids hear our church's mission, vision, and values all the time,

and it makes a difference in how they view the church—and on a much broader level, it shapes how they view God's work in the world.

When our kids go to church, they don't hear a message that's different from what we've taught them. We want them to understand and embrace Pastor Rod's heart. It's good for them, it's good for their parents, and it's good for our team and me.

We often invite key leaders of the church—pastors, board members, and volunteers in other ministries—to join us so they can see what God is doing in Kids Ministry. They love to sit in the back to watch our volunteers serve and the Spirit change lives.

Work hard to help kids make the transition to youth ministry.

To smooth the way for our fifth graders to make the move up to junior high ministry, I ask our youth pastors to preach to our kids several times in the months before the move. I also ask the youth pastors to be the evangelists for our fourth and fifth graders' retreat every year. At these events, the youth worship team leads the singing. I want our fifth graders to know, love, and trust the youth pastors before they officially move up and walk through their doors. To make the transition even more comfortable, a couple of us from Kids Ministry often go up to speak or lead a game for the kids in junior high. We want them to see that we're a family—a supportive one, not a dysfunctional one.

One Body

When I had tunnel vision, I felt isolated and angry. I had to acknowledge, though, that I'd created the silo where I was living. I had been living with a chip on my shoulder, and I dared anyone to say a word about it. I'm not the only one who has struggled with this perception. The church in Corinth was full of factions and cliques. Some claimed to follow Paul, some followed Peter, and some followed Silas. When Paul wrote them to address this problem, he challenged them to see things very differently. They were all of one body, the body of Jesus Christ. They all had different roles, personalities, and experiences, but they were all meant to function as an entire, healthy, strong body.

> Now, instead of ignoring Pastor Rod and the other ministries of our church, I want our Kids Ministry to celebrate them. We're partners, not competitors.

Now, instead of ignoring Pastor Rod and the other ministries of our church, I want our Kids Ministry to celebrate them. We're partners, not competitors. This isn't just good organizational strategy; it's good for my soul, too. My anger has subsided, my relationships have improved, and we share a common vision to help people in our church and our community love Jesus Christ. It's a beautiful thing.

Think about it...

1. How have you seen a leader's tunnel vision have negative effects on a team?

2. Have you ever been a leader or team member in a silo? If so, what happened?

3. What are some practical steps you can take to avoid tunnel vision?

"My senior pastor just doesn't get it." 8

Nobody has to tell me that I live in a dream world. I'm completely convinced that's the case. As I talk to kids' ministry pastors and leaders around the country, I often hear them say, "Brian, I love working with our kids and volunteers, but our senior pastor really doesn't understand what we're doing." But mine does. Pastor Rod was a children's pastor before he became a senior pastor. He loves kids and completely understands what we're trying to do. In fact, he offers resources before I even ask for them! Not long ago, he came into our main room and announced, "Let's completely redo the stage." He then offered suggestions for ways to make it cool and fun.

I responded, "That would be great, but we just changed it—completely—a few months ago." I had to talk him out of investing more in our stage. Strange problem, huh? And I remember the day when he walked into my office and put a new computer with the latest software for video editing on my desk. I hadn't asked for it, but he anticipated a need and met it before I made a request. I can't imagine a senior pastor more interested and invested in kids' ministry.

Pastor Rod's heart is so much with us that he sometimes tells people, "Someday, I'm going to end my time in ministry the same way it began. I'd love to go back to working with kids." I'm not so sure I would be willing to give my job up for him, but I'm absolutely convinced he means exactly what he says.

Many people who lead children's ministries feel a bit schizophrenic. They're thrilled to be involved in reaching kids and shaping their lives, and their best friends are their partners in kids' ministry—but they feel like they're working on an isolated island, disconnected from the other ministries in the church. They're sure their senior pastor values their contribution, but he doesn't really know what's going on each week in the lives of kids and volunteers. His attitude, they're sure, is "Thank you for taking care of the kids so I don't have to think about them." These pastors value the kids' ministry as one of the best marketing tools of the church. If parents know their kids are loved and taught well, these parents are far more likely to attend and tithe. That's absolutely true, and there's nothing wrong with this perspective—but it's incomplete. Kids' pastors and leaders want to feel like they're a valued part of a team, not just a promotional tool to grow the church.

In many churches, members of the pastoral staff view the kids' ministry as a glorified baby sitter that provides good spiritual input. In the most painful situations, the pastor and the staff see kids' ministry leaders as nuisances who ask for too much. The message to these children's leaders is "No, you can't have more resources. We've given you plenty, so make it work. And stop asking for so much! Can't you see we're busy doing real ministry?"

That hurts. It really hurts.

But the tension sometimes goes beyond the lack of organizational information and resources. At a conference for kids' ministry leaders, a lady asked to talk to me privately. We found a quiet place in a room where no one could overhear us. Almost in tears, she said, "Brian, my pastor doesn't care about our ministry, and he doesn't know a thing about me. He hasn't asked me any questions about what motivates me, what encourages me, or what frustrates me. He doesn't know where I've come from or where I'm going. To him, I'm just a cog in his machine to make the church grow."

I asked, "Have you tried to get to know him?"

Her eyes got wide and she leaned forward. She glared, "I'd never tell him anything about my personal life. I don't trust him."

"Why?" I asked.

"Because I've seen it before: When he gets personal information about someone, he uses it as leverage to control people. I'm not willing to take that chance." She took a deep breath, and then continued, "He's broken confidences and told people things he should have kept to himself, and believe it or not, he's even used some information shared in private as sermon illustrations!"

I probed, "Are you sure?"

"Brian," she almost snarled, "He did that with something I told him when I became the leader of the children's ministry. I talked to him about a problem I was having with one of the parents, and he used the story the next week in his sermon! He didn't use names, but a number of people knew who he was talking about. It ruined my relationship with those parents."

Her situation is very painful. I'm amazed that she can continue to work in an environment where trust has been eroded. It's a testimony to her commitment to the Lord, to the kids who come each week, and to her team of volunteers. But her situation is an extreme. The vast majority of senior pastors are wonderful people who love God and care for people, but feel the pressure of juggling all the demands of running a church. In these churches, children's ministers feel like the solenoid in a car engine. The pastor is like the average driver, and the car is his vehicle to get to his goals and fulfill his vision. Most drivers crank up their cars and drive along without having a clue what a solenoid does. They've heard of it, and they know it's important, but they only notice it when it's broken and demands attention. In the same way, many senior pastors only notice the children's ministry leader when something's broken. When that happens, they want it fixed as quickly as possible so they can get on the road again. I'm not trying to be harsh or critical. Senior pastors have tons of responsibilities, and they have very little training in children's ministries. These two factors can cause them to pay attention to kids' leaders only when there's a problem. They take them for granted the rest of the time. These kids' pastors don't feel valued as people, they don't feel understood, and they don't believe the pastor even wants a relationship with them. That's sad, and it's painful, but it's the reality in a lot of churches.

Of course, most senior pastors feel offended if someone suggests they aren't deeply concerned about all their leaders and every ministry in the church. They insist, "Of course I care for our children's ministry leader!" But if you ask the leader, he or she often says, "I guess my pastor is too busy to ask about our ministry or me. As long as we take care of the kids, he's happy with us." Most senior pastors make assumptions about the way children's ministry pastors feel about them and their relationship, but assumptions usually lead to big misunderstandings.

Even in the best situations, problems can occur between a children's pastor and a senior pastor. I know. It happened to me. Several years ago, poor communication between Pastor Rod and me led to wrong assumptions, which eventually produced suspicion and distance. As we drifted apart, I assigned motives to him that were, well, negative. These ideas festered in my mind because I didn't walk into his office and say, "Hey, we need to talk." Instead, I let my vain imaginations run wild. They almost led to a disaster.

At the time, I'd been working at First Assembly for almost five years. I couldn't put my finger on any reason for the distance between Pastor Rod and me, but it was clear, strong, and increasing. In the middle of my growing resentment, I received a phone call from my good friend, Brian Massey, who I consider to be a wonderful, creative partner. I'd enjoyed working with him for several years at The Oaks Fellowship. We had always joked that one day, we'd work together again. Over the years, we continued to stay in touch. When he called, he told me about the situation at The Oaks. Their Kids Pastor had just resigned, and they were looking for someone to fill that role. As soon as I heard his story, I immediately began to think, *Wow! I've been feeling distant from Pastor Rod lately. Maybe this is God's answer!*

Interesting analysis, huh? I assumed God wanted to solve the problem in my relationship with Pastor Rod by giving me an escape hatch. I couldn't admit it at the time, but later, I realized that pride was driving my desires. When Brian told me about the opening, I immediately envisioned myself walking into The Oaks in a triumphant return to be the hero who came back to save the day in the kids' ministry! What a clear, powerful image! What a jerk!

Feeling vindicated and strong, I told Pastor Rod about the opportunity for me to leave our church and return to The Oaks. Of course, I explained the "signs from God" that were leading me in that direction. (In his grace and self-control, he didn't laugh at my stupid rationale in ascribing my selfish motives to "God's will." He's a very kind man.) But I could tell he was hurt. He didn't understand why I wasn't happy at First Assembly, and he didn't understand why I would even consider leaving. He asked some honest, probing questions to see if there was anything wrong, but I wasn't very transparent with him.

I left his office, but I knew something wasn't right. I'd been less than honest with him, and I had to come clean. That night I went over to his house. I explained that one of the main reasons I wanted to leave was that our relationship wasn't as close as it had been. I announced, "I don't think you want me around anymore, so it seems like a good thing to leave."

Pastor Rod was surprised at my assumptions. He told me how much he appreciated me, but he didn't stop there. He posed a very important—and soul-piercing—question: "Brian, why do you think you're feeling that way?"

I thought for a minute, and finally I spoke. I had to admit, "It's not your fault. I'm not sure what happened, to be honest with you. You've gone overboard to convey your appreciation for me. You've given me every opportunity to grow as a leader, and you've valued me as a friend and partner in ministry." In fact, he had recently asked me to preach in all of our Sunday morning services while he was on a mission trip. I'm not aware of a church our size where the senior pastor allows the kids' pastor to fill his pulpit on Sunday morning in his absence.

When the blinders of wrong assumptions fell away from my eyes, I realized Pastor Rod had been pouring into my life and trying to build our relationship. But I hadn't done my part—not even close. I was depending on him to do it all. I was making the severe mistake that so many kids' ministry leaders make.

> When the blinders of wrong assumptions fell away from my eyes, I realized Pastor Rod had been pouring into my life and trying to build our relationship. But I hadn't done my part—not even close.

My mistake: Ignoring my responsibility to develop a healthy relationship with my senior pastor.

There was, in fact, distance in my relationship with Pastor Rod, but in our conversation that night, I soon realized it wasn't his fault. I had to own it. I'd ignored my responsibility to maintain open, honest communication with him. I had expected him to do all the work. When—eventually and inevitably—he didn't meet my expectations, I blamed him. After all, he's the boss. He's responsible to take the initiative in our relationship, isn't he? No, every relationship is a two-way street.

As I travel around the country, speaking to kids' pastors and volunteers, I hear some of them say, "My senior pastor doesn't get me," "I'd love to do some big things for our kids' ministry, but my pastor doesn't share my vision," or "If it weren't for my senior pastor, I'd love serving at my church." These statements concern me and break my heart, but they also make me wonder if these kids' ministry leaders are making the same mistake I made.

After the debacle with Pastor Rod, I made a vow that I would work hard to make sure our relationship grew healthy and strong. I stopped depending on him to take the initiative, and I determined to cut short any wrong assumptions about his motives. If I sensed any confusion or strain of any kind, I was going to bring it up so we could resolve it without delay.

Senior pastors don't come in "one size fits all." They have different life experiences, different gifts, different personalities, and different visions for their churches. But in regards to their relationships with kids' ministry leaders, some principles apply in virtually all cases. Here are some commitments I've made, and I recommend every kids' leader make them in this important relationship:

I pray for my pastor and his family daily.

As the distance between Pastor Rod and me grew, I seldom prayed for him. Now, I've made a commitment to pray every day for him: for his walk with God, for wisdom in leading our church, for the spiritual vitality of his family, and for God's protection for him as he steps out to make a difference in our church, our city, and the world. Praying for him causes me to appreciate him even more.

I own my pastor's vision.

It's important not only to understand your pastor's vision, but also to *own* it, emotionally and volitionally. For our Kids Ministry to play a vital part in our church, I needed to be in step with my pastor's heart and take the initiative to coordinate everything we do with his vision for the church. Wrong assumptions and resentment kill a spirit of cooperation. Clearing out the gunk in my mind and heart enabled me to embrace Pastor Rod's vision. Now, his vision has become my vision, and we're partners again—in fact, more than ever.

What does this look like? When Pastor Rod became the Senior Pastor at First Assembly, God led him to elevate the importance of soul winning. In almost every sermon, he uttered statements that communicated this passion. He said (and still says), "A soul is a soul is a soul is a soul," and "Every soul matters to God." I began teaching this perspective to our volunteers and kids. It was a core value of our church, and it became a core value to our Kids

Ministry. And our kids have gotten it. When we talk about God's purpose for their lives and our church, they often blurt out, "Pastor Brian, don't you know? Every soul matters to God!" Yeah, I know, and I'm glad they know, too.

I understand I'm a servant—first to my Senior Pastor and then to the church.

I'm the Kids Pastor at First Assembly because my Senior Pastor believed in me enough to give me the privilege and responsibility of serving the children and parents of our church. If it weren't for his vision for kids and parents, this ministry wouldn't exist. Without his faith in me, I'd be somewhere else.

If you have a leadership role in your church, you're in the same privileged position: Your pastor believes in you. He may not be the most supportive or informed of any pastor on earth, but he has given you one of the most important platforms in the life of your church. Savor it. Let it sink deep into your heart so you appreciate the honor. Never allow someone in the congregation to drive a wedge between you and your senior pastor by creating suspicion. Your senior pastor deserves staff members who will stand beside him with integrity and loyalty. This doesn't mean you have to be in the very best situation, but you have to trust that God has you in the position, you can serve him gladly, and you value your pastor's vision and heart.

> This doesn't mean you have to be in the very best situation, but you have to trust that God has you in the position, you can serve him gladly, and you value your pastor's vision and heart.

I look for opportunities to serve.

It's a mistake to sit on the sidelines and demand that your pastor take the initiative to get you involved in other aspects of church life. If your pastor is anything like Pastor Rod, he'll seldom ask for your help because he doesn't want to burden you. There are, however, plenty of needs in the church that could use your expertise and help. He would appreciate you volunteering to help, especially if it's in an area that has nothing to do with kids' ministry.

I realized that I could serve Pastor Rod by caring for his family. When his boys were in school, he traveled extensively to raise money for missions. Cherith and I volunteered to help Tyler and Parker with all kinds of science and art projects. I also still try to check in on Pastor Rod's wife, Cindy, when he's out of town. It's a small thing to make a call to see if she needs something, but Pastor Rod seems relieved to know that we're there for her while he's away.

When I travel with him, I listen and watch to see if I can help in any way. I can carry some of his bags, make a quick call to check on our next meeting, or help with travel arrangements. I'm not brown nosing to earn points. I do these things so that he can focus on more important things.

I try to read between the lines.

When Pastor Rod became the Senior Pastor at First Assembly, I had a goatee. Pastor Rod sometimes joked with me about it and laughingly threatened to shave it off. I assumed he was just kidding around. As he spoke at a conference for pastors, he explained that he refuses to impose his preferences on his staff. He said, "I prefer our pastors be clean shaven, but I have several of them who have moustaches and goatees. I'm not going to force them to shave."

He didn't know I was in the room that day, so I was sure he wasn't giving me backhanded directions to shave my goatee. But I got the message. His kidding had been a subtle (obviously too subtle for a dense guy like me) message that he preferred me to shave my goatee, but I'd missed it.

When we got home from the conference, I made plans to shave it off. But I wanted it to go out with a bang. We had scheduled a fundraiser, and people contributed over $1000 for me to shave my goatee. Of course, my real reason for shaving wasn't to raise money. That was just an added benefit. I wanted to honor the preference of my pastor.

On another occasion, I asked him how he wanted me to dress for an event. He said, "I'll be in a coat and tie, but you can dress how you'd like." He meant it. He wasn't demanding that I conform to his expectations, but it was obvious that he believed the event was important. I wore a coat and tie.

Working with Pastor Rod on a project.

Because Pastor Rod and I have a relationship based on trust and respect, I'm happy to honor his preferences. It's not a pain, and it's not a strain. It's just another way to serve the person God has called to lead me.

I offer accountability instead of forcing my pastor to require it.

I don't know of any senior pastor who enjoys tracking down any member of his staff to check on him or confront him when there's a problem. In my relationship with Pastor Rod, I was determined to *offer* accountability instead of forcing him to *demand* it from me.

When I came to First Assembly, Pastor Rod asked me to email him any time I had a problem of any kind that needed his attention. In my pride and self-protection, I didn't want to admit that I had any problems (at all), so I didn't send him any emails about needs or difficulties. One day, he found out about an incident in the Kids Ministry. He was perplexed to hear about it from someone besides me. When he called me into his office, he had to be an investigator, trying to find out what happened, instead of a partner, helping to resolve it. My silence had forced him into this role.

Don't make your pastor play CSI. Take the initiative to tell him anytime there's a problem he needs to know about. When you're going to be late, call. When something goes wrong, tell him. When there's a problem that's going to affect other ministries, give him a heads up.

I immediately inform him of job offers.

Let's not pretend. Sometimes, the pastor of another church calls and says, "We have a position as Kids Pastor open. Do you know anyone who might be interested?" What he actually means is "We need a Kids Pastor, and I was wondering if *you're* interested."

I get these calls and emails from time to time. When I get an offer to leave First Assembly and go to another church, I immediately email Pastor Rod and let him know about it. I don't want him to hear it from someone else (senior pastors talk) and wonder if I'm considering leaving. A commitment to inform him clears away any misunderstanding and builds trust. And if I ever leave, he'll appreciate being in the middle of the conversation from the beginning.

I'm committed to be open to correction.

For years, my insecurity caused me to struggle with being defensive. Under the hurt feelings and protests is a deep sense that I'm not adequate, personally or professionally—or both. No one is above correction, and we can all learn to handle it with grace. Sometimes, I do a pretty good job of controlling my outward appearance when someone criticizes me, but I'm dying inside. When this happens, Pastor Rod's perception kicks in. He tells me, "You've done a great job in controlling the tone of your voice and looking relaxed while you're defensive."

> No one is above correction, and we can all learn to handle it with grace.

He nailed me. When I bristle from correction, I need to look into my heart to see what I'm trusting in. I can then choose to thank God for his love and grace, and I can accept the correction as a gift instead of a threat.

Here's the principle: When your actions are corrected, it doesn't mean your character is being questioned. Chill out and learn from the challenge instead of defending yourself to the death!

I need to keep my frustration quiet.

Complaining may be a person's favorite sport, but it can poison a staff team and other relationships. In children's ministry and church work, there's always plenty to gripe about, and I'm good at it! Whining to a sympathetic ear feels good for the moment, but it causes a lot of damage to everyone involved. I've seen it too many times, so I've made a commitment to communicate my frustrations only and always to the appropriate person. When I have a complaint, I go directly to Pastor Rod and talk to him. I don't talk to board members, parents, volunteers, or other staff members. And when others are taking shots at Pastor Rod, I don't smile and nod to confirm their complaints. I tell the person, "I understand you're upset, but I'm not the person to talk to. You need to go to Pastor Rod (or whoever is the right person). Okay? Okay."

I want to defer praise to God and others.

Like every other human on the planet, I love compliments. I need to be careful, though, to deflect praise appropriately to God and to others who have contributed to a successful event. When someone says, "Brian, that was a great sermon," I say, "I have an amazing teacher." If they say, "I sure am glad you're on our staff," I respond, "I'm so pleased to serve an amazing leader who allows me to work alongside him. It's one of the great privileges of my life."

We need to be shrewd when people compliment us. Most of the time, they sincerely mean every word they say, but some people use flattery to drive a wedge between us and our pastor or people on our team. They build us up to tear them down. Don't let this happen. I'm always Pastor Rod's ambassador. When I visit someone in the hospital, I begin the conversation by saying, "Pastor Rod wanted me to drop by to see you."

And, of course, we need to give honor to Christ for every success. He's the author and perfecter, the Alpha and Omega. It is the highest honor and deepest privilege of our lives to serve him and see him use us to change lives. When people tell me I've done a good job, I say, "Thank you so much. It's such a privilege to serve God and see Him work."

I may disagree with Pastor Rod in private, but not in public.

In any working relationship, people have different opinions and plans. It's happened plenty of times in my relationship with Pastor Rod. Not long ago, we talked about a problem in our Girls Club Ministry. I believed we needed to do one thing, but he saw it a different way. He patiently listened to my point of view, but it was his decision, and he didn't pick my solution. When I walked out the door and into the meeting with the Girls Club Coordinator, I didn't say, "Hey, here's the decision, but it's Pastor Rod's, not mine. Actually, I was on your side. I wanted to help you, but Pastor Rod insisted we do it his way." Instead, I represented the decision as ours. I said, "This is what *we* decided is the best course of action."

Don't throw your senior pastor under the bus just to earn points with others.

Communicate, communicate, communicate.

When I communicate well with Pastor Rod, even difficult times seem to work out because we're honest and we trust each other with the truth. But when I fail to communicate with him, even good times can produce doubt and resentment. I've made a commitment to let him know anything and everything I think he needs to know. I send him email updates on meetings

I'm having. I see him or email him if there's a significant problem. If a schedule change might affect him or others on our staff, I keep him in the loop.

Most of the time, these notes are simply FYI. He doesn't have to respond, but he wants to be informed. The last thing he needs is to be blindsided by a situation I should have told him about. Don't excuse poor communication with statements like "I didn't think it mattered," or "I didn't want to bother you." Let him decide what bothers him. What's the worst thing that could happen? He could hit delete. But more often, he gets information that prevents frustration, and your willingness to communicate builds trust. Not bad results.

Fight the thought: "If only I was in charge."

Some of us daydream about being in charge. We're sure we know how to handle the church better than our pastor. Think again! If we knew the stress, anxiety, and enormity of each decision (and know that each decision we make affects the livelihood of the entire staff and congregation), we'd have a new appreciation for our pastors.

> Some of us daydream about being in charge. We're sure we know how to handle the church better than our pastor. Think again!

Being a senior pastor is one of the most demanding jobs in the world. The financial, organizational, spiritual, and relational strains are enormous—but they often carry the burdens alone. They don't whine to us, and they don't even tell us about all the problems.

Take my word for it. You don't want that responsibility. It's easy to be an armchair quarterback when the results of your second-guessing don't affect anyone. To be honest, most of our confidence that we'd have done a better job is 20/20 hindsight. If your pastor had the ability to see the future, his calls would be 100% right all the time, as well. If you live in a dream world that you're smarter and wiser than your pastor, it's time to wake up and be thankful you don't carry those burdens.

I don't make negative assumptions about his motives.

When we disagree with a pastor's decisions, it's easy to ascribe sinister motives to him. We think he's stupid, or selfish, or manipulative. We see signs of pride or fear. Sometimes, we're assigning our own hidden motives to him. Psychologists call it *projection*. We need to nix that. Our pastors are doing their very best. Certainly, they make bad choices from time to time, but we can assume they're doing all they can to honor God and lead with integrity. If we're going to make assumptions, let's assume our pastor has the very best motives.

I tell the whole truth the first time.

Since we're talking about motives, we need to be honest about what's going on in our own hearts. Sometimes, we exaggerate the good things to look a little better to impress people, and we downplay the bad things so we don't look so foolish. Both of these are, in fact, lies. Partial truths are also partial lies, designed to "save face" by giving enough truth to avoid outright lying but not enough to expose our stupidity and sin. Tell the truth—the whole truth, the first time. It saves a world of trouble.

I scheduled a meeting with one of our team members for 10:00 in the morning. At ten minutes past that time, he wasn't there, so I called him. He said, "I'm on my way. Be there in a sec."

I could hear his television in the background, so I knew he was still in his apartment. When he arrived, I asked him about it. He explained, "I'd forgotten about our meeting. When I saw your name on the caller ID, I started walking toward the door as I answered. So, technically, I was on my way." His answer didn't do a lot to build trust in our relationship.

One of my Kids Ministry leaders was supposed to make a bunch of phone calls for me. After a few days, I asked, "How are those phone calls coming?"

She replied, "I haven't talked to everyone yet."

When I pressed her on it, she admitted she hadn't tried to call anyone. She tried to convince me she'd told the truth that she hadn't "talked to everyone yet," but I carefully explained that her statement was purposely misleading.

In our relationships with our senior pastor (and everyone else, for that matter), we need to tell the whole truth the *first* time. If your pastor is as sharp as Pastor Rod, he'll ask questions that he already knows the answers to in order to determine if you're telling the whole truth or not. It's a lot better to tell the truth than to develop the reputation of being a liar.

I express heartfelt appreciation.

Some kids' ministry leaders tell me they really enjoy working in their church with their pastor. I ask, "When was the last time you told him?" For some, it's very recent, but others admit it's been a long time.

Don't just be thankful—express it in a way that communicates your heart.

For appreciation to be received, it must be sincere. Don't just go through the motions and hope it works out okay. If you're not feeling thankful, take time to pray. Ask God for eyes to see what He sees so you can overlook some of the difficulties and really appreciate the phenomenal opportunity to reach kids for Christ in your church.

In the past few years, I've tried to make gratitude a normal part of my communication. I send Pastor Rod thank you notes for all kinds of things and, even more, for being a terrific leader and friend. Sometimes, I give him small gifts to show my appreciation. I want him to know that I don't take him for granted. Notes, words, and gifts let him know I'm very thankful for him, and these things help keep our relationship strong.

The Doctor Is In

I'm a slow learner. Some people learn vicariously, but I have to learn from the hard school of failure. When I failed to communicate with my pastor, I invited a world of trouble on myself, on Pastor Rod, and our team. My false assumptions almost ruined one of the most positive and powerful relationships in my life. But thankfully, I've learned a thing or two from my mistakes.

> My false assumptions almost ruined one of the most positive and powerful relationships in my life. But thankfully, I've learned a thing or two from my mistakes.

If you're struggling in your relationship with your pastor, take some time for an accurate diagnosis. First ask, "Is it me? Am I contributing to the problem in some way? If I am, what am I doing that's causing the problem?" Look over the principles in this chapter and give yourself a grade to see how you're doing—and don't grade on a curve! Be ruthlessly honest with God and with yourself about what you see in your response to your pastor.

If you've been making a good-hearted effort to communicate well and be supportive of your pastor, but it's still not working out, ask, "Is this where God wants me to serve?" Before you give up on your current role, take the initiative to talk to your pastor to have a good conversation about his perception of his vision, your role, and how you can work together more effectively. Your fundamental question is "Pastor, how can I help you more?" If a significant, long-term problem exists, you might then say, "Pastor, it seems that our relationship isn't as strong as it should be. I feel disconnected. Is that just me, or do you feel the same way?" Let him answer. You might find out that he thinks everything is going great, or you may realize he feels just as distant in the relationship.

Before you meet, ask God to give you ears to hear and patience to listen. Don't accuse and don't demand. Listen to his heart as well as his words. You may find that you've missed each other for a long time, and this conversation gets you back on the same (or close to the same) wavelength. But you may realize the role isn't a good fit for you, and it's time to do something else, either in the church or at another church.

In an honest conversation with your pastor, there are no guarantees. Your responsibility is to be humble but assertive, to speak the truth in love, and to offer a path toward a better relationship. But you can't force it. If you feel hurt, you need to forgive. Forgiveness is unilateral, but reconciliation takes both people taking steps to build trust with each other. Forgive and make the offer and then see if God works to begin building a relationship of trust and respect. It's a wonderful thing when it happens.

Remember your ultimate goal and the One you serve. In Paul's letter to the Colossians, he wrote, "Whatever you do, work at it with all your heart, as working for the Lord, not for human masters, since you know that you will receive an inheritance from the Lord as a reward. It is the Lord Christ you are serving" (Colossians 3:23-24). In this part of his letter, he was writing to slaves. If slaves could make the choice to serve their masters "as unto the Lord," we can serve our senior pastors with all our hearts with the promise of a great reward. This doesn't mean you're locked into a dysfunctional relationship with a pastor who doesn't value you. All of us need to try our best to resolve difficulties in this relationship. If it's too destructive, however, we need to trust God and go somewhere else.

There's nothing noble in staying in a sick, destructive environment. But it's not good, right, or fair to resent a leader without making every effort to resolve differences and find common ground. No situation is perfect. Let me give you a word of advice: Don't put unrealistic expectations on your pastor or the church. We don't need perfect leaders or churches, but we need *good enough* situations where we can serve God with all our hearts. If you know God has called you to that place at this time, learn to overlook some things, communicate well and often, and give everything you've got to the Lord, the kids, the parents, and the volunteers in your ministry. And God will smile.

Think about it...

1. Describe your relationship with your pastor? What are the strengths? What causes frustration (for both of you)?

2. In your role as kids' leader, how do you feel (thrilled, valued, used, neglected, etc.)?

3. Look at the list of principles in this chapter. Which ones are you doing well? What are the positive results you see?

4. Which ones need some work? What specific steps will you take to implement one or two of them? What can you expect to happen? Is it worth the effort?

5. Do you need to have an honest conversation with your pastor about your role? How will you prepare for it? When will you have it?

"I can't see a thing." 9

In October 2003, I picked up Pastor Rod at the airport. He was return-
ing from an event at the Assemblies of God National Center for the Blind
(NCB). On the drive home, he told me that the NCB was involved in a
number of exciting ministries, including translating *The Book of Hope* into
Braille, making audio books for blind children, and printing Sunday school
literature for visually impaired adults. As he talked about each one, God
gave me a heart for this ministry.

A week or two later, Pastor Rod and Cindy were out of town again, and
I volunteered to take their son, Parker, to school each morning. Parker has a
big heart for missions, and he has raised a lot of money for a number of projects. On the way to school, we talked about the possibility of raising money
for the National Center for the Blind. Both of us were excited about it, and
we began concocting some plans.

This wasn't my first rodeo. I'd done all kinds of crazy stunts to raise
money for missions. For different projects, I'd dyed my hair, submerged myself in chocolate (I *hate* chocolate, by the way), and even lived on top of a
billboard for an entire week. This time, I wanted to do something that would
be more dramatic than anything I'd ever done before. As Parker and I rode
in the car, we had an amazing idea: I would live as a blind person all day,
every day for a whole week.

It seemed like a great idea, and I thought it would be easy to pull off. I was so wrong. I talked with many of those who are blind in our church and our community. Two of my blind friends, Johnnye Pryor and Anita Miller, spent hours talking with me and helping prepare me for the week of blindness. The more I talked to them, the more I realized the challenge I was facing. I met with Dr. Hampton Roy, an eye surgeon, who attended our church, to figure out the best method for me to shut out all light for a week. I also wanted to know if this hair-brained scheme might permanently ruin my vision. He assured me that a week without sight wasn't going to be a problem. There was, however, a very different concern. Could we find a way to completely block out every ray of light for a week? Dr. Roy had spent his life giving sight to the blind. No one had ever asked him to reverse course and take sight away from someone with perfect vision. He had lots of ideas. We tried contacts, simulating the eyesight of someone legally blind. It blurred everything beyond recognition, but I could still make out objects and shapes. I wanted total blindness. We tried the dark glasses doctors prescribe when a patient has eye surgery. They darken everything, but they still allow the person to see. Finally, I found a website for scientific studies of light deprivation. A company had invented goggles that were comfortable but blocked out 100% of the light, rendering the person totally blind. They were perfect, so I ordered a pair.

When I told the kids about the projects to help blind people and the idea for raising money, they caught my passion. Immediately, they began raising money and receiving pledges. They were excited to tell people their kids' pastor was going to be blind for a week to raise awareness about these needs. Many of them asked their parents to take them to local businesses and neighborhoods. They worked very hard, and they received a lot of pledges of support.

Soon, the day came for us to kick off "Hope for the Blind." At the end of the second service, two local television stations brought crews and anchors to tell our story. The kids were excited to be on television! As I stood on the stage, I reminded the kids about our purpose: to share the gospel of Jesus Christ to those who are blind. I read a passage of Scripture: "If we confess our sins, He is faithful and just to forgive us of our sins, and to cleanse us from all unrighteousness" (1 John 1:9). Then I put on the blinders. The last thing I saw was the Bible. At that moment, I began a life-changing experience—one I hadn't anticipated at all.

It was an amazing week. The kids at our church had a goal of raising $10,000. By the end of the week, they had raised over $19,000 in cash and pledges. It was a wonderful success in fundraising, but God wasn't limited to a single purpose. In all of my planning and preparation the weeks before it began, I hadn't imagined the impact this experience was going to have on my life—physically, emotionally, and spiritually. There were some hints, however, before I put on the blinders. In a staff meeting the week before the fundraiser, our team studied a chapter in a book. The author uses a term that caught my attention. He says many Christians suffer from "blind complacency." They develop a habit of resisting God, refuse to change, and eventually don't even notice the Spirit's

In all of my planning and preparation the weeks before it began, I hadn't imagined the impact this experience was going to have on my life—physically, emotionally, and spiritually.

promptings. This condition, he writes, is worse than knowing what needs to change and not changing it. It's a condition of resistance and refusal that has become permanent. It's so pervasive that the person doesn't even notice God's voice anymore.

Pastor Rod explained that God often uses a progression of events to get our attention. First, the Holy Spirit whispers to us. If we don't respond to His whispers, He tries to get our attention through circumstances—usually painful ones. If we still don't turn to Him, He sends someone who has the courage and love to speak the hard truth to us that we have to change . . . or else. If we ignore all three, we develop the hard-hearted trait of "blind complacency." In the staff meeting that morning, I wasn't sure these concepts applied to me, but I hoped some other people in the room were listening!

Later, I realized God had orchestrated this conversation to prepare me for the upcoming week. The days of blindness weren't just to raise money for blind people, and they weren't only to teach kids at our church about giving sacrificially. Another purpose was to use blindness to open my eyes to one of the biggest mistakes of my life.

The blinders completely blocked out all light. They were specially made to suck up against a person's face so no light could penetrate. I knew I wasn't going to be able to do a lot of things I normally did each day, but there was one thing I could still do: I could pray. I asked God to reveal Himself to me and give me insight about my life. I had no idea how much He wanted to answer that prayer!

As I spent time with God, He showed me a huge area of blind complacency in my life. I'd depended on my gifts and talents so much that I could "wing" almost any event. I prepared for my talks, but not like I should have.

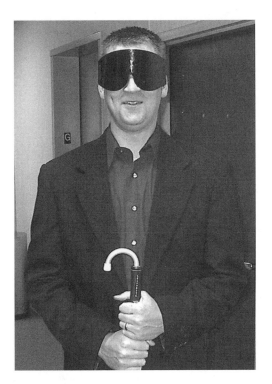

I often walked into important meetings without a thought about God's purpose for the discussion. I'm pretty quick on my feet, so I assumed I could make it work on the fly—and most of the time, I did. During this week, though, God showed me that winging it demonstrates disrespect for Him, for the people I lead, and for the kids in our ministry. The pattern of my life—my values, my attitude, and the way I led people—had been hindered by a huge blind spot. Now, something had to change.

This startling insight was revolutionary news to me, but I quickly realized I was the only one who hadn't seen it. I groped my way into Pastor Rod's office to tell him what God had been showing me. Maybe, it's a good thing I couldn't see the look on his face. He listened patiently, and then he told me he had tried to point this out to me on many occasions, but I had ignored him. Instantly, I remembered several conversations when he had warned me about trusting too much in my ability to wing it. Each time, I blew him off. I was convinced he was wrong. Suddenly, God finally opened my eyes to the truth, and I realized just how blind I'd been.

A thousand instances came to mind. I'd walked into meetings and come up with plans on the spur of the moment. I had made important decisions without stopping to pray. I'd laughed at people who were disciplined and said, "They're so rigid!" I read very few books, and I didn't bother to learn from national experts on kids' ministry. When I attended conferences, I spent more time visiting with friends and networking new contacts than going to the sessions to study and learn important principles. I was coasting, leaning on my natural talents and abilities to get me through each day.

My mistake: Being blind to my weaknesses and flaws.

When the Spirit of God finally shines a light into the recesses of a person's heart and reveals the gunk that's been there for a long time, he has several options: He can turn off the light, he can grovel in shame about how bad he's been, or he can man up and take steps to change the direction of his life. Suddenly, I was faced with these choices, and I was determined to man up. During the long week of blindness, I let the new reality sink in. I felt genuine sorrow and shame, but not the kind that leaves us empty and dirty. I cried out to God for forgiveness, and He showed up.

By the end of the week, I was very thankful God had opened my eyes, but I wondered why it had taken so long. It would have been a lot better if I'd listened to Pastor Rod all those times (or *any* of those times) he had spoken the truth in love.

I'd been blind to my complacency, but people can be blind to almost anything: bitterness over unresolved past hurts, a sense of entitlement that they deserve God and people to treat them a certain way, the drive to be a success, laziness, the demand for a comfortable life, the need for approval, a critical and judgmental attitude, nagging behavior, and many other problems. When God or people try to point out these blind spots, they often ignore them or ridicule them. Blind spots make them feel completely justified in their destructive behavior and negative attitudes. Until God breaks in, they stay stuck for a long, long time.

> Blind spots make them feel completely justified in their destructive behavior and negative attitudes. Until God breaks in, they stay stuck for a long, long time.

Lessons from the Darkness

During the pivotal week of darkness and in the months after it, God taught me some of the most valuable lessons of my life:

I learned what it meant to be "shut in with God."

Even though I was blind, Pastor Rod and I felt it was a good idea for me to take my normal role of leading praise and worship on Wednesday night. I stood in front of everyone, but I wasn't able to see the audience, so I couldn't tell if the people were following my lead. Suddenly, I felt alone in the presence of God, and I began to sing for an audience of One. The liberty and love I sensed at that moment amazed me. I forgot other people were in the room. I connected with God in a rich, deep way, and I truly worshipped like I hadn't done in a long time.

Sometimes, God gives us an experience of His presence that's unforgettably intimate and intense. It can happen at a youth camp, at a revival, or at home, alone or with members of the family. In that wonderful moment, we forget about everything around us and worship God with no reservations. Our experience is like King David's when he danced before the Lord and didn't care what anyone thought.

That night showed me what I'd been missing in my worship of God. I'd taken Him for granted, but not any longer.

I learned that I'd been blind much longer than I realized.

As I prepared for the week of blindness, I asked God to open the eyes of my heart. As I closed my physical eyes, I asked Him to let me see Him as He really is—and let me see myself clearly, too. God answered my prayer *big time!* He showed me that I'd been complacent about Him and my role for several years.

I had always been proud that I could adapt to any situation and make it work. No matter what problem surfaced, I could find a solution on the fly. I thought, *Man, I'm good! I can figure things out anytime, anywhere.* There's nothing sinful or evil with being a quick-witted person—unless that talent takes the place of dependence on God. Over the years of ministry, I'd elevated winging it to an art form. In fact, I ridiculed people who valued planning. When someone asked me about the next steps we should take, I would laugh and respond, "I don't care, and I don't want to know. God will show me when the time comes for me to make that step." But that was a cop-out. I just didn't want to plan because it didn't showcase my ability to come up with answers at a moment's notice. And planning was work. I was too lazy to work that hard.

As I looked back on the way I'd lived and led, I had to face the hard fact that the patterns of complacency and laziness had been the dominant factors of my life for a long time.

I learned new meaning to the biblical concepts of blindness.

Throughout the Bible, blindness and darkness are used to teach important spiritual truths. When I experienced blindness, I had a far better understanding of the power of these concepts. The Bible talks about the people living in spiritual darkness. Now, I understood the emptiness and helplessness of spiritual blindness. My world was dark, boring, and lonely, and it was frightening. I couldn't connect with people; I had no color and excitement. Many times each day, I felt confused and lost. People who live without Christ share the same experiences.

When I took off the blinders, the words of the hymn, "Amazing Grace," rang in my head: "I once was blind, but now I see." In a new way, I had a deeper understanding of the light of Christ in His love and forgiveness.

Paul tells us, "We live by faith, not by sight" (2 Corinthians 5:7). During the week when I wore blinders, I realized that I had to trust God and people more than ever. I realized that the circumstances of life—the things we can see—aren't the whole picture. God is at work behind the scenes, in light and in darkness, to accomplish His will. Even when I don't know what He's doing, I need to trust Him. I also learned to trust the voice of people who gave me direction. Most people were very attentive and helpful, but a few either weren't paying attention or had a sinister streak because they led me into doorframes. (Those things are surprisingly hard!)

I learned to give thanks for the small things in life.

We may not really appreciate God's gifts until we don't have them. During the week of blindness, I missed seeing my wife's and my kids' faces. I could hear them, but I missed the twinkle in their eyes and the smile on their faces. I also soon realized I had no idea what time it was. I couldn't see my watch, and I couldn't tell where the sun was in the sky. I think people got tired of me asking, "Hey, what time is it?"

I learned to appreciate the kindness and abilities of others.

I'm an independent guy—proud of it, too. I don't ask for help because I don't think I need it. But as I groped along during the week I wore blinders, I would have been completely lost if it weren't for those who possessed a gift that I didn't have: sight. I had time to reflect on this insight, and I realized God had put a lot of wonderful, loving, talented people in my life. I'd taken them for granted, but not anymore. I may have overlooked them in the past, or in some cases, I'd been jealous of a person's glowing abilities, but now, I began to value the contribution each person made—to me, to God, and to the kingdom. We're all part of the body of Christ, with different gifts God wants to use to reach out and build up. Finally, I began to appreciate the role others play.

Kindness became even more valuable to me when I felt particularly disconnected from others. Sometimes, when I was talking to a group of people, one of them would walk off, but I would continue to talk to people, thinking she was still there. Another person would inform me, "Uh, Brian, she's not here anymore." I felt a little embarrassed and hurt. And even if people didn't leave, I soon realized I was missing something I'd always taken for granted:

I couldn't see people's gestures or facial expressions, so I couldn't read their unspoken messages. Several people could tell I was getting frustrated, and they took extra care to communicate with me and include me in conversations. I really appreciated their kindness.

When you're in need, true friends rally around you.

I guess it goes without saying that the person who sacrificed the most that week was Cherith. She selected my clothes, moved furniture out of my way, picked up toys and clothes the kids left on the floor, drove me to meetings, brought me every meal, cleaned up my messes, and waited on me hand and foot. And she never once complained. I marveled at her love, and one day I asked her, "Can you imagine what it would be like if I had an accident and you had to do all this every day for the rest of our lives?"

She immediately and sweetly answered, "Brian, you know I'd take care of you."

Each day of blindness, our entire church staff pitched in to help. John Van Pay, our Student Pastor, gave me rides to work. Randy Jumper, our Young Adults Pastor, checked my email for me. My assistant, Debbie Tollett, was a constant help in the office. And all the staff ladies mothered me all week to make sure I had everything I needed.

But they wouldn't be my team and my friends if they didn't have some fun at my expense. All of them are kindhearted, loving people, but they couldn't pass up a golden opportunity to give me a hard time. In our staff meeting that week, they asked me to tell a funny story that had happened to me some weeks back. I got into the story, laughing about it and describing every detail. When I finished, I wondered why no one was laughing. As I talked, they had all gotten up, one by one, and left the room. They got me on that one, but they weren't finished.

One day at lunch, several of us were riding together to a restaurant. I was in the back seat listening to everyone talk. Suddenly, the driver jammed on the brakes and everyone screamed! For a split second, I thought we were all dead, and I panicked . . . until I realized our Business Administrator, Reta Russell, had orchestrated the whole thing. She just wanted to see my reaction. That's two.

One afternoon later in the week, I tried to show everyone that I'd gained confidence in my ability to get around on my own. As we were coming down the office hallway, our Evangelism Pastor, Tommy Covington, asked, "Hey Brian, do you need me to help you find the door?"

I assured him, "No way, man. I've got it."

As we approached the door, Tommy went through first. I thought he would at least hold the door, but he took me at my word and *smash!* The door hit me right in the face. Three paybacks are coming.

To this day, I don't know who the culprit is, but when I was sitting at my desk in my office all week, someone came and stood next to me without saying a word. I could hear him (or her) breathing, and I demanded, "Who is that?" But all I got was silence—until the person arrived mysteriously again the next day for another round of torture.

I'll get that person back one day. Count on it.

Shining a Light in the Darkness

One of the most difficult—and important—tasks people face is addressing the blind spots in their lives. Many people live their entire lives in darkness about their flaws because they're unwilling or unable to shine a light in the dark places of their hearts. It takes a lot of courage to be honest instead of defensive, but the benefits are incredible. Here are some suggestions:

> It takes a lot of courage to be honest instead of defensive, but the benefits are incredible.

Ask God to open your eyes.

Spiritual darkness requires spiritual light. A friend of mine talked to a man in his church about a blind spot in his life, and the man responded, "I don't have any blind spots." That's ridiculous. All of us have blind spots. We all have negative attitudes and patterns of behavior we've excused for years. But we can't deal with them on our own. We need to ask God to give us eyes to see the truth and the courage to take steps to deal with it. No matter what our blind spot may be, we begin by asking God for His light.

Listen to God's voice.

We have blind spots because we've discounted the Spirit's whispers and ignored the signs and circumstances He's put in our path for many years. Now, it's time to listen. How does God speak to us? There are many ways He can get our attention. He uses the power of His Word, the nudge of the Spirit, the honesty of a friend or mentor, or the shock of sickness, failure, or death to get our attention.

The problem isn't God's inability to speak, but in our unwillingness to listen. We may have ignored His voice because He tells us things that make us feel uncomfortable. If we stick our fingers in our ears too long, we stop hearing Him at all—and that's really scary.

Develop a sensitive ear to hear God's voice. Ask Him to lead you to passages of Scripture that speak to your need and expose your blind spot. Pay attention in prayer to sense His leading. If you're willing to listen, God will speak to you. You can count on it.

Listen to people you trust.

Make an appointment with your pastor, your mentor, your spouse, or someone else who is wise and has your best interests at heart. Swallow hard and ask, "Do you see any areas in my life where I might have a blind spot? Are there flaws or weaknesses I haven't dealt with?"

The person may be shocked at your question, so give him a minute or two to answer. Then listen. Don't explain the observation away, don't excuse your behavior, and don't be defensive. Remember, you asked the question. You asked because you trust this person's honesty, wisdom, and love. After you've listened for a while, ask a second question: "Is there anything you've noticed in my life that you've been afraid to tell me because I might be too defensive?" And listen again.

Clearly identify your blind spot.

Don't generalize the problem. When the diagnosis is unclear, the prescription isn't targeted or effective. Take time to think, pray, and talk to a friend until you have a clear handle on it. Don't just call it "a bad attitude." Dig down to uncover the long buried feelings and expose the actions. You might want to define it as "difficulty trusting people," but a

Don't generalize the problem. When the diagnosis is unclear, the prescription isn't targeted or effective.

little investigation (by you and the Holy Spirit) might show you that you're unwilling to trust people today because you haven't resolved deep wounds from the past. In this case, present behavior has a past cause.

Look for resentment, the demand to control others, self-doubt, fear, the compulsion to live for the approval of others, laziness, or any other problem you may have excused for so long. Call it by name and deal with it ruthlessly. Don't sugarcoat it or skirt the issue. Identify it, and tell someone you trust how it has affected you and your relationships.

Take a positive approach.

Some of us wallow in our flaws in the hope that if we feel really rotten long enough, we'll eventually feel better about ourselves. Has that ever worked for anybody? No, I didn't think so. The grace of God is boundless and free. We aren't defined by our sins and our painful pasts. We are loved, chosen, adopted children of the King! He is for us, not against us. He knows we're nothing but dust, and He's not shocked when we confess we've had a blind spot for many years. Instead of focusing on how bad we've been, we need to set our thoughts on God's wonderful purpose for our lives. We're far more motivated when we focus on developing a new way of doing things rather than spend our mental energies trying to control the pain of the past.

Let me give you an easy example: Many people fail in dieting because they spend their time thinking about not eating food. The result—they daydream about eating, so they eat more instead of less.

In *The Psychology of Winning*, author Denis Waitley writes, "One of the best guarded secrets is the kind of self motivation practiced by high achievers and effective leaders . . . it is imperative to concentrate our thoughts on the condition we want to achieve, rather than try to move away from what we fear or don't want."[1] In other words, winners focus on the solution rather than the problem.

Write down your growth goal.

Vague intentions almost never take us to a desired destination. It's not enough to define the problem. We then need to ask God for a vision of what it will be like to live in freedom without the blind spot. When you define the goal, write it down, describe the benefits, and trust God to take you there. Many people struggle with the description of the goal because they're afraid the price they'll have to pay isn't worth it. It is! The best encouragement to move forward is a clear picture of the finish line. Go into detail. How will your ministry look? How will your family relationships benefit? How will you experience financial peace and freedom? How will you take advantage of new opportunities?

If you can define and describe your goal in writing, you're well on your way to eliminating the blind spot. A good plan is essential. Solomon wrote, "A wise man thinks ahead; a fool doesn't, and even brags about it" (Proverbs 13:16 NLT).

Define manageable steps toward your goal.

Some of us quit because the task seems too big, too challenging, and too hard. If, however, we break a goal into reachable steps, we can make remarkable progress. We can also be naïve about what it takes to change. Enthusiasm is a good beginning, but it won't take us very far on its own. I know. I've tried. If I had tried to get up early each morning to do a workout routine, read a hundred books a year, read the Bible through every month, and pray two hours a day, I'd have gotten pretty discouraged! I need to have big goals but manageable steps toward these goals.

In 1968, John Naber aspired to be an Olympic swimmer. He had trained for years and had achieved a fast time . . . but not fast enough. By his calculations, he would have to trim four seconds off his best time, but he had four years to qualify for the 1976 Olympic Games in Montreal. Four seconds may not seem like much to you and me, but to Naber, it seemed impossible. He had trained every day for twenty years, and his best time had hit a plateau. He realized if he trained ten months a year for the next four years, he needed to trim one-tenth of a second each month in order to qualify. When he broke his goal into manageable parts, he believed he could make it—and he did. He won four gold medals at the 1976 Summer Olympics, each in world-record time.

If a swimmer can use the principle of graduated steps toward a goal to achieve a gold medal or two (or four), you and I can take bold, incremental steps forward with the power of the Holy Spirit.

No Excuses

Excuses are perpetual blinders. With them, we can stay stuck for a lifetime. When we find the courage to open our eyes to the truth, amazing things can happen. To make real change a reality in our lives, we have to be get rid of every excuse we've used in the past.

Excuses are perpetual blinders. With them, we can stay stuck for a lifetime. When we find the courage to open our eyes to the truth, amazing things can happen.

Excuses aren't unique to people today. When God called Moses, he had all kinds of reasons he couldn't step up and be the leader of God's people. God told Moses he was the one who would lead the Israelites out of captivity in Egypt to the Promised Land. Here are some things Moses said to God:

> But Moses said to God, "Who am I, that I should go to Pharaoh and bring the Israelites out of Egypt?" (Exodus 3:11)

> Moses answered, "What if they do not believe me or listen to me and say, 'The Lord did not appear to you'?" (Exodus 4:1)

> Moses said to the Lord, "O Lord, I have never been eloquent, neither in the past nor since you have spoken to your servant. I am slow of speech and tongue" (Exodus 4:10).

Moses was full of excuses why he couldn't obey God's leading. He's not alone. For years, I made tons of excuses. I convinced myself I could wing it and fake everyone out, so I didn't need to change. For a long time, the difference between Moses and me was that he was willing to make the sacrifice to see growth, and I wasn't.

We all have our favorite excuses. We use them to either consciously or subconsciously keep ourselves from having to face the hard truths in our lives. Let's look at some of the most common excuses people use to avoid dealing with blind spots:

"I'm comfortable the way things are, so I don't really need to change."

Change requires courage. It's a lot easier to tell ourselves, *Everything's fine. No problem.* We rationalize our problems, and we actually convince ourselves this is the way we want to live. That's what alcoholics and addicts do.

We can roll along for years until we come face to face with the damage our behavior has caused in the life of someone we love. Then, we have a choice to make.

"I'll probably fail, so I won't even try."

The challenge of making a substantial change in our lives can look like an insurmountable mountain. We look at the ingrained habits we've created and the people we've hurt and conclude that it's not worth the effort to try. We may have seen others try and fail, and we don't want anyone to laugh at us. It's a lot easier to give up before we even start.

No, it won't be easy, and yes, people have tried and failed. But we certainly can't succeed if we don't give it our best shot. The question is "Is it worth it?" What are the benefits in our walk with God, our self-confidence, our relationships, and our career? We don't want to do it alone, and we don't have to. We need a running partner, someone who will tell us the truth, pick us up when we fall, and not listen to our lame excuses.

"It'll take too long to change."

The process of real change certainly takes time. In fact, everything worth achieving requires determined effort. We live in an instant society, and we get what we want at the blink of an eye. But life transformation doesn't happen at 4G speed. The metaphors of spiritual growth in the Bible are agrarian: plowing, planting, watering, weeding, and finally, the harvest. Should we expect anything different in our spiritual growth?

I understand that it can be hard to keep your game face on 24 hours a day. On some days, we come up short in the motivation department. We need two valuable traits: patience and persistence. Patience is the willingness to endure misfortune or pain without complaint; persistence is the tenacity to hang in there until a goal is reached. We won't make it very far without plenty of stops to refuel our engines with encouragement and refreshment.

Start Now!

It's time to eliminate your excuses and your rationalizations. Make a declaration: I'm not going to live by my excuses any longer! After Moses had given God multiple reasons why he didn't want to obey Him, he said, "O Lord, please send someone else to do it" (Exodus 4:13). As it turns out, all of his excuses were only smoke screens. The real issue was that Moses didn't want to do what God had called him to do. Is that you? Have you been making excuses to cover up the fact that you're unwilling to do what God has called you to do? It's time to be honest. Be honest about your blind spot and trust God to change your life.

A repentant heart is essential. Wise friends who speak the truth are worth more than gold. A good plan marks the way forward. But we won't make any progress at all until and unless we take the first step.

A repentant heart is essential. Wise friends who speak the truth are worth more than gold. A good plan marks the way forward. But we won't make any progress at all until and unless we take the first step. We can look at our plans and tell ourselves, *That's a good idea. I'll work on it later.* But we'll always find another excuse tomorrow and the day after that and the day after that. In his book, *Walking with God*, John Eldredge writes about choosing between action and procrastination:

> These simple moments of decision are filled with significance. When I choose to avoid whatever it is God has brought up, something in me weakens. Something feels compromised. It is at least a refusal to mature. But it also feels like a refusal to step toward God. Thankfully, the opposite is true. When I choose to face the uncertain, admit the neglect, or enter into my fears, something in me grows up a little bit. I feel strengthened. The scales tip toward a closer walk with God.[2]

James tells us that faith without action is worthless. You'll never be able to make the changes God has revealed to you unless you take the first step. Are you ready? Take some time to think and pray about the principles in this chapter. All of us have blind spots, but not all of us are willing to bring light into the dark places of our lives. I hope you will. Prepare your heart to hear from God. Listen for His gentle whisper. Open His Word and let His Spirit guide you to passages you may have read dozens of times, but maybe this time, they'll speak to you like never before. As you hear from Him, you'll be tempted to discount, rationalize, blame, minimize, and excuse yourself. Don't do it! Find the courage to be honest with God and then tell a trusted friend what God has shown you.

This isn't an exercise for the faint of heart, but then again, it's not an exercise for only a few of us. All of us need to have an open heart like David when he prayed:

Search me, God, and know my heart;

    test me and know my anxious thoughts.

See if there is any offensive way in me,

    and lead me in the way everlasting (Psalm 139:23-24).

When I was finally honest about my blind spot, I experienced God's love and presence more than ever before. I found a new sense of freedom and joy, and I discovered a new level of love in my relationships with Cherith, our children, and everybody in our ministry. As I look back, I have to wonder, *What took me so long?*

Are you ready?

Think about it...

1. What are some blind spots you've noticed in people's lives? Why haven't they been honest and courageous in dealing with them?

2. Has God shown you a blind spot in your life in the past few years? What did you do when you saw it?

3. Has the Spirit whispered to you as you read this chapter? Are you eager or afraid to hear Him?

4. What is your next step (or first step) in dealing with the blind spot in your life? Who can help you?

"I can't try that!" 10

Like every other children's ministry leader in the country, I've always been on the lookout for great curriculum. For years, I ordered material promoted in magazines and everything my friends recommended. Some of it was pretty good, but I was often disappointed. After a while, I decided to give a shot at writing our own. It worked out pretty well! Our volunteers liked our home-grown curriculum, and the kids responded to it. Pastor Rod, always deeply invested in our ministry, told me numerous times, "Hey Brian, this is great stuff. Why don't you package it for other churches? They'd love to use it!"

I blew him off. It was fine for me to write for our church, but who was I to write kids' ministry curriculum for other churches? This perspective sounds noble and humble, doesn't it? It wasn't. I was afraid of failing, but even more, I was terrified of putting something into the national market-place and being criticized.

Psychologists say that the fear of rejection is the most common and most crippling fear. The fear of failure is its first cousin. We fear failure because it leads directly to the risk of criticism and rejection. I wasn't willing to take that risk, so I hid behind false (but very convincing, I'm sure) humility.

I often talked to our volunteers and kids about being courageous for God, but I was a coward. From the first time I wrote curriculum and saw

God use it to change young lives, I got messages from all sides—Pastor Rod, parents, volunteers, and the Holy Spirit—to produce the material for a national audience. They were very encouraging, but I refused to listen. After three years, I think God had heard enough excuses. One day, Pastor Rod and I were on our way to the hospital to visit some people. We were talking about something supremely deep and spiritual, like where the new Bass Pro Shop was going to be built. Suddenly, he turned to me and said, "Brian, the material you're writing for our Kids Ministry is awesome. You really need to produce it so other churches can use it."

I gave him my normal excuses: "You really don't know what you're saying. Kids' curriculum has to have first class videos, great material, and terrific marketing. I can't do that."

He didn't blink. "Sure you can."

I shook my head and got quiet, but his confidence began to make a dent in the steel shell of my excuses. For the next year and a half, I kept writing material for our ministry, but the conversation with Pastor Rod stayed stuck in the back of my mind.

One day, I saw an ad for some new, hot children's curriculum. It was advertised as the latest and greatest thing, so I bought it. The kit cost about $400. When I reviewed it, I was very disappointed. I thought, *Our team could do better than this.*

At that moment, the Spirit of God almost shouted at me, "Then why aren't you doing it?" (I waited for Him to say,

> At that moment, the Spirit of God almost shouted at me, "Then why aren't you doing it?" (I waited for Him to say, "What's it going to take, you moron?" But I don't think God calls people names like that.)

"What's it going to take, you moron?" But I don't think God calls people names like that.)

I called our team together, and I explained that we were going to write and produce curriculum that could be used by other churches. We were going to do it right: take time to write well, produce excellent videos and printed material, and test it before we rolled it out. Over the next several months, we worked like crazy, and we had a blast!

I spoke at a kids' camp the next summer, and we offered the new material to the kids' ministry leaders who were there. About a dozen of them bought it, and in a few months, they gave me very encouraging feedback. They liked it! They told their friends in other churches, and I got more calls and orders. I put the material on our church's web site, and even more children's ministry leaders ordered it. It went so well that we decided to produce another set of materials.

People might look at me and think I'm a natural risk-taker, but that's a misperception. Other people might have thought my ideas were off the wall, but I never did anything I wasn't sure would succeed. On the outside, I looked like a wild-eyed day-trader, but inside, I was terribly risk-averse. Yes, we had The Plagues Tour, the Easter egg hunt, and dozens of other outlandish events, but this time, I never did anything I wasn't absolutely sure would be a slam dunk success. Producing this curriculum threatened me to the core because there was a genuine risk that I'd fall flat on my face—and be laughed at by the people I respect. I'd heard people criticize nationally known material, and I'd been one of the chief critics. I sure didn't want to have to take my own medicine! In addition, I realized that once material is produced, it's out there for a long, long time. If I wrote crummy material for our church, I could toss it in the trash that afternoon and move on. But if I wrote crummy material and published it, my reputation could be tarnished for years.

As we saw God bless our material and we were able to use the proceeds to pay for the next rounds of curricula, I began to gain confidence that God was really in this. (Yes, I'm pretty slow. You don't have to tell me.) All of the materials were being sold by viral marketing: friends telling friends to call us. One day, my friend, Kelly Presson, stopped by the church and said, "Hey, why aren't you advertising in *Children's Ministry Magazine*?"

"Uh, because it costs $2700 for an ad."

He wasn't buying my reasoning. "Yeah, but you'd be able to pay for that with only a couple of dozen sales. It's worth it. You'd be crazy not to."

Now, I was catching flack from my friends for not marketing enough! We put an ad in the magazine, and God opened even more doors with kids' pastors from around the country. It's been amazing, but I almost missed it all because I was paralyzed by fear. Writer Frederick Wilcox notes, "Progress always involves risk; you can't steal second base and keep your foot on first base."[1] I'd kept my foot on first base way too long. When I finally took a risk, God blessed far more than I ever could have imagined.

For years, I'd lived in fear. If I couldn't guarantee success, I wasn't willing to try anything new and different. I might try a new curriculum someone else had written, but if it wasn't good, I didn't take any heat. I'd lived in a carefully constructed comfort zone and avoided any risk of

> For years, I'd lived in fear. If I couldn't guarantee success, I wasn't willing to try anything new and different.

failure and rejection. But that's not really living. Finally, God pushed me to face my fears and try something new, and I'm so glad He did.

My mistake: Allowing fear to keep me from taking risks.

What's Yours?

Risks come in all shapes and sizes for kids' ministry pastors and volunteer leaders. We can try a creative outreach to kids in our communities, host a workshop for parents, connect with local school administrators, take initiative to network with other children's ministry leaders in town, make announcements in church, or pray out loud with volunteers. Why don't we step up? Because we're afraid nobody will show up, someone we trust will let us down, or we'll look stupid in front of our peers. There are dozens of reasons, but they all keep us from being the leaders God wants us to be.

Fear is a reality in all of our lives. If you say you don't have any fear at all, either you're a liar or a psychopath—neither of these is a good option! Some of us can't admit our fears because they're so terrifying we can't face them. Denial, though, never leads to growth, peace, joy, love, and strength.

When we talk about fears, some people immediately think of things like spiders, tornados, heights, mad dogs, snakes, falling, and cramped spaces. Some people have bizarre fears. I saw a television program about people who feel overwhelmed with the fear of change. No, not changing relationships and circumstances. These people are afraid of *change*: dimes, nickels, pennies, and quarters. When a psychologist held up a penny, a lady freaked out!

We all experience normal, healthy fears. In a crisis, our fears trigger adrenaline and enable us to be more alert and energetic to face the problem. These fears, though, aren't long-term problems that ruin our lives.

Another kind of fear can cripple us. In fact, the command, "Fear not," is the most common directive in the Scriptures. In his book, *If You Want to Walk on Water You've Got to Get Out of the Boat,* John Ortberg notes, "The single command in Scripture that occurs more often than any other—God's most frequently repeated instruction—is formulated in two words: Fear not."[2]

Why does God command us not to fear? It doesn't seem like the most serious issue in the world. In fact, fear doesn't show up in the Ten Commandments or the list of the Seven Deadly Sins. No one ever gets removed from ministry or receives church discipline for being afraid. So why does God tell people to stop being afraid more often than He tells them anything else? It's because fear is the number one reason people avoid obeying God.

Fear causes a wide range of physical, emotional, relational, and psychological damage. It puts a straightjacket on us so we don't do what God has called us to do. It's a wet blanket on our emotions and keeps us from experiencing joy and the adventure of walking with God. It causes us to compare ourselves with others instead of loving them. When we're doing better than them, we're arrogant; when they look better than us, we feel ashamed. It's all about us! Living with this kind of fear eventually causes psychological and physical strains—and even burnout.

> Living with this kind of fear eventually causes psychological and physical strains—and even burnout.

Fear is a barrier between us and the things God is calling us to do. It keeps us still when God wants us to move, keeps us quiet when God wants us to speak, and causes us to shrink back when God wants us to reach out. Strong, creative spiritual leadership isn't satisfied with the status quo.

Leaders don't focus on excuses for inaction; they look at possibilities for God to do amazing things. But leaders often have to overcome their fears. Abraham left everything he had known to follow God into a distant land. Moses had been tending sheep so long that he lost confidence in his leadership abilities, but God still had a mission for him. After his initial hesitations (I can relate!), he marched boldly into Pharaoh's presence and demanded, "Let my people go!" Joshua and Caleb believed God to lead the people into the Promised Land and conquer giants even when others cowered in terror. David put down Saul's armor and faced the colossal giant, Goliath, with a sling and five stones.

Courage isn't the absence of fear, but the willingness to take action in the face of fear. Every leader has to face very real fears. Don't you think Abraham wondered a few times why he was leaving the comfort of home to risk his life and his family in a foreign land—for a God he couldn't see? I can imagine Moses had plenty of second thoughts about God's crazy plan to free slaves with a stick that turned into a snake. And David might have wondered, *What'll happen if I miss the big guy's head?* The heroes in Hebrews 11 and throughout the Bible were just like you and me. They wrestled with their fear, too, but they didn't let it conquer them.

How can we address this problem? Some people pretend not to be afraid. They talk big, but they aren't fooling anyone. Others redefine it. They claim, "I'm not afraid. I'm just being very careful." In his book, *Next Generation Leader*, Andy Stanley compares "careful" and "fearful":

Careful is cerebral; fearful is emotional.

Careful is fueled by information; fearful is fueled by imagination.

Careful calculates risk; fearful avoids risk.

Careful wants to achieve success; fearful wants to avoid failure.

Careful is concerned about progress; fearful is concerned about protection.[3]

As you look at this comparison, are you fearful or careful? Be honest. Before I finally found the courage to step up, fear dominated my life far more than I could admit.

Facing Our Fears

The Scriptures give a lot of encouragement to face our fears because it's so common—so human—to let them control us. One of the most powerful passages is from a letter by Paul to his protégé, Timothy, a young pastor at the church of Ephesus. Paul encouraged him not to let others intimidate him because of his youthfulness. Timothy was afraid of being inadequate. I can identify with him. I remember being a twenty-two-year-old kid coming out of Bible school. Even though I'd been working part-time at a church as a staff pastor for three years, I, now, had the role full-time. It was official, and it was daunting. I didn't feel like an adult, much less a pastor. I was sure people were looking at me and whispering to each other, "How is this guy going to be our spiritual leader? He's just a kid!" I was paralyzed by the fear of making the wrong decision and being second-guessed by everybody in the church. I was filled with anxiety about being a young pastor—just like Timothy.

> The Scriptures give a lot of encouragement to face our fears because it's so common—so human—to let them control us.

In his second letter to Timothy, Paul reminds Timothy, "God has not given us a spirit of fear, but of power, and of love, and of a sound mind" (2 Timothy 1:7). What is Paul saying? Crippling fear doesn't come from God. Instead, God pours out the solution to fear: power, love, and a sound mind. Let's look at these.

Power

Many people want power, but they seek it from the wrong sources. They look to money, fame, titles, or the ability to manipulate others. These people are controlled by the fear that someone else has more than they have, so they never find contentment. The power Paul is talking about is very different; it's spiritual power. He wrote the Ephesians about this kind: "Now glory be to God! By his mighty power at work within us, he is able to accomplish infinitely more than we would ever dare to ask or hope" (Ephesians 3:20 NLT). The power to face our deepest fears doesn't come from possessions, positions, or people. It comes to humble hearts that trust God to provide wisdom and strength.

Love

The Apostle John wrote a lot about love. In fact, he identified himself "the one Jesus loves." In his first letter, he describes the nature of God's love: "There is no fear in love. But perfect love drives out fear, because fear has to do with punishment. The one who fears is not made perfect in love. We love because he first loved us" (1 John 4:18-19). The unlimited, unconditional, and unmerited love of God gives us incredible confidence. We don't have to prove ourselves or hide our flaws. He knows everything about us, and

> God doesn't spare us from pain. He promises to be with us in the middle of our difficulties, and He assures us that no pain is ever wasted.

He loves us anyway! We didn't earn His affection by being cool or smart or good-looking. We didn't earn it at all. It's a free gift of grace that came at a high price. As Paul wrote the Christians in Rome, "God demonstrates his own love for us in this: While we were still sinners, Christ died for us" (Romans 5:8).

God's love produces confidence and the courage to conquer our fears. How? When we understand the depth of God's love, we're not afraid of anything this life throws at us. His love for us is greater than anything that would come against us. Paul later told the Roman believers, "For I am convinced that neither death nor life, neither angels nor demons, neither the present nor the future, nor any powers, neither height nor depth, nor anything else in all creation, will be able to separate us from the love of God that is in Christ Jesus our Lord" (Romans 8:38-39). God doesn't spare us from pain. He promises to be with us in the middle of our difficulties, and He assures us that no pain is ever wasted. He uses it to teach us life's most valuable lessons and prepare us to have a greater impact on others.

A Sound Mind

Fear thrives on faulty thinking. The origins of many fears are thoughts that have grown out of control. Negative, critical, self-defeating thoughts may come from painful memories. Some of us hear "tapes" of past conversations for years. But the enemy of our souls also plants condemning ideas in our minds. We think they're logical and reasonable because they come from our own thought processes, but they're straight from hell. Some translations of 2 Timothy 1:7 list this third component as "self control" or "self discipline." This implies the control of the crazy thoughts and fears that enter our minds.

King Solomon wrote, "Better is he that rules his spirit than he that takes a city" (Proverbs 16:32). Controlling our thoughts in a healthy way takes work, but self-control focuses our minds on God's grace and power, which produces courage. Most of us have one or two recurring thoughts that fuel our fears. It may be a fear of criticism, a fear of failure, or even a fear of success. These thoughts have controlled us too long. They've limited our potential, ruined our relationships, stolen our happiness, hindered our faith, and kept us from experiencing God's best in our lives. It's time to do something about it.

Practical Steps

In a letter to the Corinthians, Paul explained how to fight: "The weapons we fight with are not the weapons of the world. On the contrary, they have divine power to demolish strongholds. We demolish arguments and every pretension that sets itself up against the knowledge of God, and we take captive every thought to make it obedient to Christ" (2 Corinthians 10:4-5). Controlling our thoughts is a fight, but it's worth our best efforts. Let me give you a few suggestions:

Evaluate your fears.

Take a long, hard look at each fear that's controlling your life. Ask yourself:

—Where did it begin?

—How has it become such a stronghold?

—What have I done to feed it?

—Is it based on something that's true or false?

—Is it something that I can do something about?

—How is it affecting different areas of my life?

Don't hurry through these questions. Take time to pray and ask God to show you recurring fears you've experienced and past hurts that might be shaping your present responses.

Downsize your fears.

Fear can take on a life of its own. When we let destructive daydreams run wild in our thoughts, they soon look like the enormous robots in *Transformers*! Bring them back down to size. You may be facing some genuine threats, but don't focus only on the negatives. Force yourself to imagine what it will be like to trust God and see Him work in and through you. Develop a sense of hope that God will come through. The person may not respond like you hope he will, and the situation may not work out like you want, but God can give you wisdom, strength, grace, and peace in the middle of it all. And you never know; God might work a miracle!

Crowd out your fears.

We have a choice about what we think about, and I'm committed to replacing negative thoughts with hopeful ones. In his letter to the Philippians,

Paul told them, "Whatever is true, whatever is noble, whatever is right, whatever is pure, whatever is lovely, whatever is admirable—if anything is excellent or praiseworthy—think about such things" (Philippians 4:8). Don't allow room for negative thoughts and fears to overtake your mind. Crowd them out with thoughts that help develop a sound mind.

Stay focused.

One of my favorite stories in the Bible is when Jesus invited Peter to step out of the boat and walk on water. As long as Peter kept his eyes on Jesus, he did fine. But when he got scared of the waves and wind, he began to sink. When we lead our ministries, we need to stay focused on the love, power, and wisdom of Jesus so we don't sink! We can expect difficulties, hard questions, and mixed motives. God never promised a smooth, easy ride. We're human, and we're going to be afraid from time to time. If we continually come back to Jesus, we'll learn to trust Him in every conceivable situation and with every person in our lives.

Playing it safe doesn't take us where God wants us to go. We don't want to take insane risks, but we need to be willing to listen to the Spirit and go where He leads us. I have to ask myself, *Does what I'm doing today require God's wisdom and power, or can I do it on my own?* My friend, Kathy Creasy, says, "It is tempting to maintain the status quo ministry—to do what we have always done, to do what others have had success doing, to do what will cause the least conflict, to do what is expected of us. But courageous faith seeks the mind of God then steps out to faithfully accomplish what God has spoken."

Risks Beyond Reason

As you face each fear and become more willing to take risks, remember an important principle: God's ideas often contradict human wisdom. We often dismiss an incredible idea He places in our hearts because it doesn't fit into our perception of what "makes sense." We discard a God-inspired idea that could change our life, our family, or our ministry simply because it goes against our logic. God speaks to us through Isaiah: "As the heavens are higher than the earth, so are my ways higher than your ways and my thoughts than your thoughts" (Isaiah 55:9).

Does your relationship with God allow Him to do things that are beyond reason? Or does His activity and direction need to fit into some neat little boxes so you feel comfortable with them? Some of us are wide open (and maybe a bit too open) to God doing the unexpected in our lives, but others are unwilling to let God be God. They assume, "This doesn't make sense, so it must not be God," and they miss out on a miracle.

Does your relationship with God allow Him to do things that are beyond reason?

The Midianites terrorized Gideon and the people of Israel. In fact, he was so scared that he tried to thresh his wheat in a winepress. The angel of the Lord appeared to him and said, "Go in the strength you have and save Israel out of Midian's hand. Am I not sending you?" (Judges 6:14)

Can you imagine receiving this message from God? The Lord told Gideon, "Go in the strength you have." What strength? He's afraid. He's a chicken. He has no strength at all. Gideon probably looked in the mirror and thought, *God, that doesn't make sense. Surely, you're not thinking I'm your guy. You'd better find somebody else.* Gideon responded with a question: "But Lord," he asked, how can I save Israel? My clan is the weakest in Manasseh, and I am the least in my family."

The Lord answered, "I will be with you, and you will strike down all the Midianites together" (Judges 6:15-16).

Gideon was full of doubt, but God eventually convinced him to take a stand to rescue his people. He took his first steps even though God's directions didn't make sense to him. But if he was thinking God's plan doesn't make sense so far, he ain't seen nothing yet!

Gideon put out a call for all of the fighting men of Israel to meet him at the spring of Harod. He needed an army to defeat the Midianites, and thousands answered his call. He looked out at this army of 32,000 men and probably thought, *This could be cool. We can do this!* But the Lord said to Gideon, "You have too many men for me to deliver Midian into their hands" (Judges 7:2).

I can almost hear how Gideon wanted to respond: "Huh? Too many men? Are you kidding me? How can you have too many men? I mean, sure, if you had 60 men in a 50-man lifeboat, then you might have too many men. But going into battle, you can never have too many men, especially if you're already outnumbered four to one. God, this doesn't make sense."

It's like God was saying, "I'm sorry, you have too much money to make it through your financial crisis," or "You have too much food to make it through the famine." What is God thinking? He explains His reasoning: "In order that Israel may not boast against me that her own strength has saved her, announce now to the people, 'Anyone who trembles with fear may turn back and leave Mount Gilead.' So twenty-two thousand men left, while ten thousand remained" (Judges 7:2-3).

219

Now, Gideon was ready to fight the army of the Midianites—not with 32,000 men, but only 10,000. Perhaps, God was done with his nonsensical orders and was ready to send Gideon's army to fight, right? Don't count on it! The Lord told Gideon to take all his men down to the water and tell them to get a drink. Those who knelt down to drink were to be dismissed from the army, but those who lapped the water like a dog were to be the only ones to go into battle. After they all drank water, only 300 remained with Gideon (Judges 7:4-7).

Gideon had to be thinking, *When is all this going to end? God, you're killing me here! I had an army of 32,000 men to take on our enemies, and now, I am left stuck with three hundred me; the only thing they have going for them is that they drink politely. God, this doesn't make sense!*

God's orders made no sense at all, from calling a scared weakling to lead the army to weeding down the army to 300 polite water drinkers. But God wasn't through yet. He gave Gideon the most outrageous battle plan that you have ever heard, and he followed the plan:

> Dividing the three hundred men into three companies, he placed trumpets and empty jars in the hands of all of them, with torches inside. "Watch me," he told them. "Follow my lead. When I get to the edge of the camp, do exactly as I do. When I and all who are with me blow our trumpets, then from all around the camp blow yours and shout, 'For the Lord and for Gideon' " (Judges 7:16-18).

Instead of rushing the Midianites in the middle of the night to attack them and kill them as they slept in their tents, God had another plan. He instructed them to hold up jars and candles and blow trumpets.

If you had been one of the men in Gideon's army, isn't this the point where you would quietly walk away? I mean, candles and jars? This is the Bath & Body Works military strategy: "All of you on aisle four, we're going to attack them with scented candles!" It doesn't make sense at all.

God's plan may not have seemed reasonable, but it was time to see if the crazy ideas were going to work:

> Gideon and the hundred men with him reached the edge of the camp at the beginning of the middle watch, just after they had changed the guard. They blew their trumpets and broke the jars that were in their hands. The three companies blew the trumpets and smashed the jars. Grasping the torches in their left hands and holding in their right hands the trumpets they were to blow, they shouted, "A sword for the Lord and for Gideon!" While each man held his position around the camp, all the Midianites ran, crying out as they fled. When the three hundred trumpets sounded, the Lord caused the men throughout the camp to turn on each other with their swords. The army fled . . . (Judges 7:19-22).

In spite of the strangest strategic concepts any leader has ever been asked to follow, God's plan succeeded. The Israelites won the battle, the enemy was defeated, and peace reigned over Israel again.

More often than not, "God ideas" don't seem to fit within the realm of our simple human logic.

—God's plan for victory in my finances: Give more to him.

—God's plan for my response to people who have hurt me deeply: Love them. Serve them. Pray for them.

—God's plan for me to have an incredible life: Die to myself.

—God's plan to become the greatest in the kingdom: Be the servant of all.

God's kingdom is upside down and inside out. From the human perspective, it doesn't make sense. "God ideas" rarely do. If your reason for not trusting God is that it seems incomprehensible, think again. Trust that the God who created the universe is far smarter than you are. If He can create the stars out of nothing, He can work miracles in your life and your situation. We may not understand all He's up to, but we shouldn't expect to keep up with God's infinite wisdom.

—I see the moment, but God sees all of time and eternity.

—I see sickness, but God sees the healing to come.

—I see broke; God sees blessed.

—I see lost; God sees found.

—I see no hope, but God sees victory.

God's direction doesn't have to make sense to us. We can trust Him because God has everything under control. It didn't make sense for Moses to stretch out his rod over the Red Sea, but God parted the sea and the children of Israel walked across on dry land. It didn't make sense for Jehosephat to put the choir out front when going into battle, yet God defeated the enemy simply with the praises of his people. It didn't make sense for Elijah to pour water on the altar three times as he battled the prophets of Baal, but God sent fire from heaven to consume the drenched sacrifice. It didn't make sense for Daniel to sleep with lions, for Shadrach, Meshach, and Abednego to refuse to bow down to the idol, or for David to carry a slingshot to battle a giant. None of these plans made sense, but God showed up each time.

If we're convinced God has given us a directive, we need to step out in faith and watch Him work. Let me put it another way: A lack of complete understanding doesn't excuse a lack of obedience. None of the people we've mentioned in these stories understood what God was doing, but they obeyed His voice and saw Him work. Similarly, you and I don't have to understand, but we have to obey.

What if? At any point in the journey, what if Gideon had said, "No way, God. Not me. Not going to do it. I'm going to stay right here and hide behind the winepress," or "I can't fight with this little bunch of men?" or "You've gotta be kidding. Candles?" If Gideon had relied on logic, he would have missed out on the victory God planned for him.

And You?

As you've read this chapter, has God reminded you of times He's whispered directions to you, but you blew Him off? Have you sensed God leading you to do something, but you found a bunch of excuses to avoid it? If you have, it's time to face your fears, take God's hand, and step out in faith. If you haven't come to that point yet, you will. Just wait. Your time is coming. No matter what our roles are today or in the future, walking with God is the adventure of a lifetime. It always involves risks, but we're never alone.

Think about it...

1. What are some ways fear cripples people, ruins relationships, and keeps us from doing what God has called us to do?

2. What fears are problems for you? How do they affect you?

3. Which of the principles in this chapter encourages you most? Which one terrifies you?

4. What are some steps you can take to downsize and crowd out your fears?

"I'll take care of that tomorrow."

11

I've always been pretty quick on my feet. When I was the volunteer Kids Ministry Pastor at Oak Cliff, I depended on my wits far too much. I was still going to college and studying for classes (well, to be honest, not studying that much), so I didn't think I had time during the week to prepare my message for the kids each Sunday. And after all, they were just kids. They liked me, they laughed at me, and I could do no wrong. They weren't exactly the harshest critics in the world!

Every Sunday morning, I pulled a book off the shelf about an hour before I spoke. I thumbed through it to find a passage of Scripture, an application point, and maybe a good story to illustrate it. After a few minutes of preparation, I was ready to go. This strategy worked week after week, until . . .

I was one of the interns at the church. Five or six of us lived in the basement of the church building. Pastor Wilson depended on us to handle any last minute problems that arose: classroom setup, leaky roof, stopped up toilet, tornado, or anything else. One Sunday morning, it had been raining hard, and we got a call that there was a major leak in the Fellowship Hall. We had to get it fixed before church. The first service was going to begin at 8:30, so we had only an hour or so to fix the leak and clean up the mess. It was a mess! We grabbed wrenches, brooms, towels, and a wet vac, and we divided the tasks. We worked like crazy to get everything ready on time. We made it, just barely, but there was a casualty: my preparation for my talk to the kids.

I ran back to my room to take a shower and get dressed. By the time I got my shoes on, it was time for Kids Church to begin. I knew I had about seven minutes while the kids were saying their pledge to the flag and we took prayer requests. I asked one of our volunteers to handle these events while I flew downstairs to grab a book and cram for my talk. In a panic, I looked at page after page. I'd already used this passage, and I didn't want to use that one. Finally, I found a passage I knew pretty well. I sprinted up to the room and started giving my talk. It was an unmitigated disaster. For thirty minutes, I flapped my gums and uttered sheer nonsense. I could read the kids' faces. They were bored out of their minds. It was a struggle to fill up the time with meaningless verbal garbage, but finally, it was time to shut up and sit down.

I was completely embarrassed. I'd been bitten by the procrastination bug—and bitten hard.

My mistake: Falling into the procrastination trap.

The Disease of Spontaneity

Isn't being spontaneous essential in kids' ministry? Isn't it one of the strengths we value? Yes, but only to a point. Sooner or later, spontaneity can become a disease that eats our best work and erodes our credibility with volunteers, parents, and staff members.

I'd made some wrong assumptions about kids' ministry. I thought all I needed was a fun personality and a great story or two to make a great message. I thought kids would absorb any-thing I gave them, and I thought I didn't have time to prepare. I was wrong about all of these assumptions.

Sooner or later, spontaneity can become a disease that eats our best work and erodes our credibility with volunteers, parents, and staff members.

In the past few years, I've studied how kids learn. I now realize it requires much more concentration and preparation to communicate spiritual concepts to minds that think in concrete terms. Enthusiasm and great stories are wonderful, but they're not enough. Kids can learn some of the most important spiritual principles, but only if we tailor our presentation to capture their hearts and minds on their level. Entertainment is only part of the equation; targeted teaching is not only possible, it's essential if we're to fulfill our calling as kids' ministry leaders. And preparation is just as important for a talk in kids' ministry as it is for a sermon in the regular worship service.

As I've talked to hundreds of people involved in kids' ministries across the country, I've observed that there's an epidemic of procrastination. We excuse it in all kinds of ways, but all our reasons lead to the same result. Yes, you have to be quick, and you never know what a kid is going to say or what kind of crazy thing will happen next. But many kids' leaders believe their enthusiastic personalities and the spontaneity of their ministry give them a license to walk in unprepared. They try to get by, doing the least they can do, and it shows.

How do I know this is true? I wrote a lesson about Easter and put it on our website. I hoped other children's pastors and leaders could use it. After Easter, I realized 50 had been downloaded between Good Friday and

Easter—and some were downloaded as late as 10:00 on Easter morning! Correct me if I'm wrong, but I don't think Easter sneaks up on anybody. Every person in church leadership knows Easter Sunday is one of the two most important days in the church calendar, along with Christmas. If it's that important, wouldn't you expect ministry leaders to make sure they're prepared?

I've heard all kinds of excuses—and I'm probably more acutely aware of them because I've used some of them myself. Here are the most common:

—Full-time kids' pastors have told me, "My week is so full of other church assignments that I don't have time to prepare my lesson until Saturday night or Sunday morning." (But I get Twitter posts, youtube links, and Facebook updates of their status in Farmville from these guys all week long.)

—Volunteer kids' pastors have said, "I work all week, so I don't have time to prepare for Kids Church before Saturday night." (I appreciate the fact that they're working a full-time job and leading this ministry, but many of them have killed hours watching their favorite shows on television during the week. Are those programs more important than the spiritual development of their kids?)

—Super-spiritual leaders have confidently told me, "Brian, I don't believe in preparing ahead because that doesn't allow the Spirit to lead me." (Really? So you're telling me that the God who knew everything about your kids before time began couldn't lead you to prepare ahead of time? Come on. Get real.)

There's no excuse for procrastination in preparing for children's ministry. God has given us an incredible privilege and responsibility to lead kids on their spiritual journey to becoming life-long followers of Jesus Christ. Someday, we'll give an account for our motives and actions. I don't want to stand before God on that day and tell Him, "I would've been more intentional about my ministry to Your children, God, but I had more important things to do."

There's no excuse for procrastination in preparing for children's ministry.

Paul wrote to the Corinthians about the day that's coming: "So we make it our goal to please him, whether we are at home in the body or away from it. For we must all appear before the judgment seat of Christ, so that each of us may receive what is due us for the things done while in the body, whether good or bad" (2 Corinthians 5:9-10, cf. 1 Corinthians 3:10-15). There are many good and noble motivations to live for Christ, to pay attention to His purposes, and to devote ourselves wholeheartedly to the work He has called us to do. We serve kids because we love God with all our hearts and He has given us a love for children. And we work hard to prepare and serve because someday we'll give an account of our lives. On that day, we want to see Him smile and say, "Well done, good and faithful servant. Come and share your master's happiness!" (Matthew 25:23)

That's what I want to hear. How about you?

Some Suggestions

I know some wonderfully gifted kids' ministry leaders who create problems on their teams because they don't prepare. One volunteer told me, "When our kids' pastor went to the bathroom every Wednesday afternoon, he always came out with his message, a game, and a skit idea. We had a couple of hours to pull all this together and make it work. We loved him, but he drove us crazy. We hoped he'd never go to the bathroom again!"

In our church's High Voltage Kids Ministry, we already have our lesson topics scheduled a minimum of six months in advance. We have service orders completed six weeks ahead. Some people might read this and say to me, "Well sure, Brian, you're in a really big church, and you have all kinds of paid staff to do all that for you." But that's not the case. I don't have a secretary. We have more than 600 kids, but there are only two of us working full-time in this ministry. If we can be this far ahead while we are writing puppet scripts, object lessons and original games, creating multiple weekly videos from scratch, and leading over 600 kids, you can do it, too!

We didn't get to this level of preparation from the beginning. Do you remember where I started? I was ashamed that I hadn't prepared for a Sunday morning an hour ahead, so I made a commitment to prepare early—on Saturday night. (Hey, that's progress. Don't give me a hard time.) Later, I realized this wasn't good enough. When I walked in to our kids' ministry on Sunday morning, none of my volunteers had a clue what was going on. They deserved better prep—and more respect—than that.

> The goal isn't just for you to be ready, but for every person on your team to be informed, equipped, prayed up, and ready to pour themselves into kids.

Create a system of preparation that works for you and your team. The goal isn't just for you to be ready, but for every person on your team to be informed, equipped, prayed up, and ready to pour themselves into kids. You might try these ideas:

—First, make a commitment to have two weeks of content prepared. Actually, this only requires you to double up the first week, so you prepare for this week and the next week. After that, you already have the next Sunday planned, so you're working on the following week's content. This way, you'll always be prepared and relaxed, and you have plenty of time to coordinate props, games, and other things with your volunteers. If you want to prepare on Saturday nights, that's fine, but you'll be working on the next week's lesson instead of the next day's lesson.

—Communicate your plans and content with your team a week ahead—at least by Tuesday. You couldn't do this when you prepared the night before, but now you can. People feel loved and valued when we let them know what's going on. Send them a quick email, give them a handout, or send them a smoke signal—it doesn't matter how you communicate, as long as you do it well and consistently. Your team then has time to study, think, pray, and plan for the upcoming Sunday content. (I've talked to lots of volunteers who love their kids' pastor, but are frustrated to death because of the lack of preparation and communication. Don't let that happen any longer. Change the culture of your team.)

—After being a week ahead for a couple of months, prepare two lessons in one week so you'll now be three weeks ahead. You may assume you don't need to do this, but it's amazing what happens when you let a message marinate in your mind and heart an extra week. You'll pray more effectively, think more deeply, and find more creative ways to connect with volunteers and kids. Try it. You'll see.

—Find a curriculum that captures hearts and communicates spiritual truth to your kids. Most of the materials on the market today are very easy to use, but many full-time kids' pastors will want to adapt content to their particular churches. But be careful: The convenience of using this curriculum isn't an excuse to wing it. Look over it two or three weeks in advance, make any changes you want to make, and then give handouts to your team so they can be informed and prepared.

Preparation Brings Peace.

Procrastination produces personal and relational stress and robs us of peace. Why in the world do we put off our preparation? I procrastinated because I didn't think I needed to prepare, I didn't think my volunteers cared to be informed, and to be honest, it gave me an adrenaline rush to live on the edge. And I'm not the only one.

I met Martha at a conference for kids' ministers. She has been a part-time kids' ministry pastor for five years. She loves it, but when she heard me talk about the need to prepare, she wanted to meet with me. She said, "I know what you mean about the kick you get when you have to deliver but you haven't really prepared. I'm afraid I'm an adrenaline junkie, too. I knew I needed to do a better job getting ready for Sunday morning, but to be honest, it always seemed like too big of a hill to climb. I know that sounds silly, but I made all kinds of excuses—and yes, I watched my favorite shows (*Grey's Anatomy* is the best!) instead of preparing. I had plenty of time. I just didn't use it. Then I heard you speak about a year ago about procrastination and preparation."

"So," I asked, "have things changed?"

She smiled, "They're starting to, but only because I have to change or I'll lose my whole team. They're sick of me running in at the last minute and racing through instructions—only half thought through—about the activities we're doing that morning."

"Caught some flack, huh?"

Martha nodded, "Big time. I lost four of my best volunteers. They couldn't take it any longer. By the time I changed, they were gone."

"Maybe you can attract some new people who will feel valued."

"Yeah," she smiled. "I sure hope so. I wish I'd heard you a few years ago, but to be honest, before the people left my team, I wouldn't have listened to you. I'd have thought you were talking to someone else."

"Did you lose everybody?"

Martha almost laughed, "No, not everybody. And those who stayed have finally told me how much they appreciate what I'm doing now to prepare the lessons a week ahead and give them information in plenty of time. I can read between the lines, Brian. They're saying I drove them crazy before!" She sighed and looked away as she almost whispered, "Why did I wait so long?"

> She sighed and looked away as she almost whispered, "Why did I wait so long?"

When I look at a lot of kids' ministry leaders at conferences, it's like looking in the mirror a few years ago. They're bright, fun, excited, and gifted, but many of them are driving themselves and their teams nuts by putting off their preparations for Sunday mornings. If that's you, don't wait until a leak interrupts your last minute prep time, and don't wait until your team abandons you in frustration. Do the work of ministry: prepare and communicate well.

Think about it...

1. What are some reasons a lot of kids' ministry leaders don't prepare well? Which are good reasons, and which are excuses? How can you tell?

2. What are some benefits of good preparation and communication with a team? Are these benefits worth the effort? Why or why not?

3. What changes do you need to make in your planning, preparation, and communication with your team? When will you make this happen?

"I can do this on my own." 12

During the week of blindness, God showed me that I'd been completely un-aware of some major flaws in my life. I faced those painful truths, and things changed. I began planning ahead instead of winging it, and I took risks I'd never taken before. As the months went along, I became confident in the new direction in my life—as it turned out, too confident. Pride again reared its ugly head. I came to the conclusion that God was lucky to have me on His side. I believed I was doing big things for God, but I somehow forgot that God, in His incredible grace, was choosing to use a flawed servant to accomplish His purposes. I thought I could accomplish almost anything on my own, and God was happy to watch and applaud.

In this season of my life, I worked hard to fine-tune my skills. I studied speaking and writing, and my talents got sharper. I was taking big risks, and great things happened. I was asked to speak at national conferences for chil-dren's pastors. I spoke to thousands at kids' conventions, and I was asked to travel overseas to train children's ministry leaders. After each talk, people came up to tell me how God had used my message in their lives. They of-ten said, "Brian, you've changed my life!" Some had a faraway look in their eyes when they said, "Man, I wish I could be just like you and do the things you're doing." It was addictive. Every success drove me to try even more new ideas, and many of them worked better than I could have imagined. I loved it, but I didn't see the danger.

Oh, I was sharp enough to know that I had to play the game. When people complimented me, I often said, "Well, praise the Lord. He deserves all the credit." But I didn't really mean it. I was certain that *I* deserved all the credit. After all, they were my ideas, my talents, my dreams, my kids, and my ministry. No one knew what was going on in the dark depths of my heart— no one except Pastor Rod.

For a year or so, Pastor Rod had been concerned about me. One time when we met to talk about our Kids Ministry, he said, "Brian, as I pray for you, the Lord keeps giving me a word."

I was pretty sure the word was "terrific," "gifted," or "amazing," so I was eager to listen.

He looked into my eyes and said, "The word is *broken*."

I laughed nervously. I had no idea what he was talking about, and I was sure he didn't either. Maybe God had gotten His wires crossed, or maybe Pastor Rod was having a bad day. As we met together over the next few months, he kept bringing up the same word God was putting on his heart: broken.

As we met together over the next few months, he kept bringing up the same word God was putting on his heart: broken.

Pastor Rod could tell he wasn't making much progress in our conversations, so he bought a book about brokenness and gave it to me. He asked me to read it and get back to him with my thoughts. I read the book as a confirmed skeptic. My attitude was *Okay, I'll read it, but it's going to have to be very convincing.*

In our next meeting, I announced, "Thanks for the book. I read it, but I don't see that it applies to me at all. I appreciate the thought, though."

Pastor Rod wasn't willing to let me blow him off, so he pulled out a bigger gun. He said, "Brian, one of the signs of a person who isn't broken is the inability (or unwillingness) to cry. I don't see you emotionally moved."

"To tears?" I asked.

He nodded. "Yeah. People who have been touched by God at the deepest level of their hearts are tender. Brian, you're not tender."

Immediately, I defended myself. "I cry. I cried when my parents divorced, and I've cried at some altar moments."

Pastor Rod could tell I wasn't willing to have an open, honest conversation, so he dropped the subject. I was happy to move on, too. I was so busy doing great things for God that I didn't have time to think about being broken. It seemed like an unnecessary distraction. I was so busy and successful, in fact, that I didn't find time to pray. God was blessing me, wasn't He? Lives were being changed, weren't they? God would understand if I put off praying until tomorrow, wouldn't He? There were too many important things to do!

I was so obsessed with doing the work of God that I neglected the God of the work. I was building the kingdom, but I ignored the King.

My mistake: Becoming self-reliant instead of trusting God to use me.

The Turning Point

God loves His children so much that He's incredibly patient, but there comes a point when He gets our attention. After living this self-absorbed way for many months, God used two people to hold up a mirror so I could see who I'd become. The picture was ugly. These were painful but essential conversations. After some hard talks with my wife, Cherith, I asked Pastor Rod if I could meet with him. I knew I had to talk with him about what was going on in my life and how messed up my heart had become.

When I sat down with Pastor Rod and told him about my conversations with Cherith, he was gracious. I explained how it had become obvious that I was far from being the man God had called me to be. My actions and attitudes were revealing that my heart wasn't right with God. He didn't say, "I told you so!" Instead, he listened carefully as I described the person I had become: self-righteous, self-reliant, and arrogant. Finally, I saw what Pastor Rod had been trying to tell me for so long, and the reality crushed me.

It was obvious this wasn't going to be a minor correction. My heart needed major surgery and rehab. In that moment, God brought to my mind the conversation Jesus had with His disciples the night He was betrayed. He explained, "I am the vine; you are the branches . . . If anyone does not remain in me, he is like a branch that is thrown away and withers; such branches are picked up, thrown into the fire and burned" (John 15:5-6). It was plain to me that I hadn't been vitally connected to the vine for a long, long time. My soul had withered, and if I didn't do something soon, I ran the risk of permanent damage to my soul, my family, and the people God had given me to serve. When I looked at myself, I saw an imminently successful

> When I looked at myself, I saw an imminently successful children's pastor, but a husband, a father, and a child of God who was an utter failure.

children's pastor, but a husband, a father, and a child of God who was an utter failure.

All of my success had provided a shell where I could hide my insecurities and fears. Now the shell was shattered, and my heart became exposed. This is what David was talking about in his most famous psalm of confession: "The sacrifices of God are a broken spirit; a broken and contrite heart, O God, you will not despise" (Psalm 51:17). I came face-to-face with all the ways I'd used people for my gain, overlooked their needs, and despised their strengths because they threatened my position as "the man."

As God showed me these sins, I went to people to confess and ask for their forgiveness. It was a long list of people. I wanted to come clean, especially in my relationship with Pastor Rod. He was, thankfully, the safest person I could imagine. I knew he loved me and would forgive me. That made it a lot easier, but it was still hard. I vomited up all the anger, resentment, and distrust I'd repressed since I'd known him. If anyone had asked me before I was broken if I had anything against him, I'd have said, "No way." But when God broke through, I had to admit a lot of sinful attitudes to God and to Pastor Rod. I was well aware that if I held anything back, this moment would be lost. I let it all pour out. I'm sure he felt a strange blend of pain and joy. He entered into the hurt I felt, but he was thrilled that God was working so deeply and powerfully in my life. It was a holy moment.

To address the problem, drastic measures were needed. I'd become a successful full-time kids' pastor, but I was a part-time follower of Christ. This had to change. I wasn't sure what needed to be done. I knew I was broken and I needed to be fixed, but I had no idea how to "fix" myself. I submitted myself to Pastor Rod's authority and told him, "Whatever you feel is the best course of action, I'm willing to accept it." To be honest, I fully expected to be fired. I was pretty sure that's how I would have handled it if someone on my team had confessed to the failures I was confessing.

After my honest and devastating meeting with Pastor Rod, he informed me that he had made a decision for me to step down from up-front ministry. There was no date set for my return. I was going to focus on my heart as long as it took to fill it with God's love, wisdom, and power. I moved from a leadership role to a support role. I didn't preach, and I didn't teach. I didn't lead worship, and I didn't lead our Kids Ministry leadership team meetings.

Does this sound too drastic? At the time, I thought it was. I wasn't sure it was the best course of action, but I knew I was messed up. I submitted myself to this decision. Looking back, I'm so glad I did.

I'm not suggesting a decision this drastic is necessary for anyone else, but it was essential for me. I'd made ministry success—and the acclaim and power that came with it—an idol that took the place of God in my heart. I had to do whatever it took to remedy the situation. To rip the idol out, I had to get to the place where I was comfortable with the thought that I might never be in leadership again.

Let God Work

In light of God's work in my heart during this time, the story of Abraham and Isaac came into sharper focus. God had promised the old man and Sarah a son and that through this son, He would bless the whole world. After 25 years of waiting, they finally had their little boy. As Abraham watched his son grow up, the child was precious to him—too precious. The promised son gradually crowded God out of the center of Abraham's heart. Isaac had become an idol. To remedy the problem, God gave a stunning order: "Take your son, your only son, whom you love—Isaac—and go to the region of Moriah. Sacrifice him there as a burnt offering on a mountain I will show you" (Genesis 22:2).

I can imagine Abraham thinking, *What? You've gotta be kidding! No way. God, you gave me this child. He's the son you promised and the one who will be a blessing to the whole world!* But Abraham didn't argue with God. He took his son on the journey to the mountain, tied him to the stone altar, and raised his knife to sacrifice him as God commanded. At that moment, the angel of the Lord appeared and stopped him. He told the old (and undoubtedly relieved) man, "Now I know that you fear God, because you have not withheld from me your son, your only son" (Genesis 22:12).

God needed to address the idolatry in Abraham's heart, and half-measures wouldn't do. He asked the old man to surrender the very thing he cherished too much. In his book, *The Pursuit of God*, A. W. Tozer communicates an important insight about Abraham at this moment of his life:

Now [Abraham] was a man wholly surrendered, a man utterly obedient, a man who possessed nothing. He had concentrated his all in the person of his dear son, and God had taken it from him. God could have begun on the margin of Abraham's life and worked inward to the center; He chose rather to cut quickly to the heart and have it over in one sharp act of separation. In dealing thus He practiced an economy of means and time. It hurt cruelly, but it was effective.[1]

I can relate. That's what God did for me, to me, and in me. He could have begun on the margins of my life to show me my selfish attitudes, pride, and love of applause, but He cut immediately to my heart. In that pivotal period of my life, God took away everything in my ministry that I had put in His rightful place. I felt totally exposed, but wonderfully cleansed.

> He could have begun on the margins of my life to show me my selfish attitudes, pride, and love of applause, but He cut immediately to my heart.

God began to matter to me—not as a tool to make me successful, but as Someone who loved me and I loved in return. Gradually, the most important thing in the world to me changed, from wanting to be the expert in children's ministry—in our church, nationally, and around the world—to wanting to be, like John, "the disciple Jesus loves." During these months, I kept a journal to help me reflect more deeply. One of the entries reads:

> I spent so much time blowing and going "in my own strength" that I wore myself to a nub and became cut off from the life-giving flow of God's presence. . . . I actually had the stupid thought that I could go ahead and handle this life and these challenges on my own. I was so busy pushing to "do" that I neglected who God wanted me to "be."

I think that's where I was, running and pushing so hard and so fast so that I wouldn't have to stop and see how cracked my character was. I was afraid of finding that out. I didn't want to believe it. Then,

I crashed and burned. And not only did I *see* it, I realized I hurt everyone around me because of it.

The awesome thing is, in the past year, God has helped me as I give in to this daily evaluation.

I'd gotten it backward. I had assumed that a right relationship with God came out of a successful ministry, but in fact, a God-honoring ministry (we let Him define "success") flows out of a rich, meaningful, loving relationship with God. Adrenaline, affirmation, and busy work in kids' ministry can't fill the gaping hole in our hearts. Only God can do that. When we neglect Him and give excuses that we're too busy to spend time with Him, our hearts wither and dry up.

The quality and frequency of our prayer life is a good indication of the condition of our hearts. When we're too busy for God and self-sufficient, we only pray to show people how spiritual we are. Oh, we might ask God to bless our efforts, but it's quick and mechanical. We don't pray because we want to be with Him, to tell Him how much we love Him, and to thank Him for the incredible privilege of being His hands, feet and voice in the lives of kids. We pray only because we want His help to make us more successful or to help us solve a current problem so we can be heroes.

Gradually, my prayer life began to change. I was thrilled God was willing to forgive all the gunk in my heart. And I was very grateful for the love, forgiveness, and support from Cherith, Pastor Rod, and some others who knew me well. As my relationship with God began to deepen, I realized more than ever that I desperately depended on Him to give me direction and to use my strengths for His honor. I wasn't willing to trust in my talents any longer. Now, prayer became essential to my spiritual life and my ministry.

I began to understand what it means to depend on God. If anyone ever could have trusted in his supreme talents, it was the Apostle Paul. He was brilliant and gifted, but God knocked him down a few notches on the road to Damascus. The Spirit changed him from a proud, angry man to a tenderhearted, dependent one. He wrote the Colossians how he viewed his dependence: "To this end I labor, struggling with all his energy, which so powerfully works in me" (Colossians 1:29). Every talent, every ability, and every opportunity are gifts from God. He is the author and perfecter of faith, and He is the beginning and the end of every ministry effort. He wants to use the abilities He has given us, and He's thrilled when we want to use them to honor Him instead of ourselves.

> Above all, I learned there's no substitute for daily, intimate connection with my Heavenly Father.

Above all, I learned there's no substitute for daily, intimate connection with my Heavenly Father. I reconnected with the vine, and I wanted His power and love to flow through me each day. But first, they had to flow *into* me. I gradually came to believe that without Him, nothing I do matters at all. My talents and gifts are worthless unless I use them for His glory and according to His power. I determined to live each day—and each moment of each day—in the loving, strong presence of God.

Has it been worth it? Far more than I can ever describe.

Changes

God has done wonderful things in every part of my life. I'm a better husband and father because I'm not wrapped up in my own successes. I'm a far better listener because my attention isn't absorbed by my goals and my wants. Things certainly aren't perfect, but I now welcome Cherith's observations that "the old Brian" is showing himself again. I'm so thankful for a wife who loves me enough to tell me the truth and help me be the man, husband, and father God wants me to be. Instead of being consumed with achieving my goals, I've put God and my family above my thirst for acclaim. It makes a difference!

In the same way, I'm a better team member and leader because I'm not manipulating people to make myself look good. I was always angling to promote myself, and I used people instead of loving them. Several people have said, "We didn't know how hard it was to work with you until you changed. It's amazing!"

I'm very grateful God has put Pastor Rod in my life. As I think back over the last few years, I'm amazed at his wisdom and love. He has been wonderfully supportive, and he's been willing to say the hard things—even when I wasn't willing to listen. I don't know where I'd be today if it wasn't for his godly influence in my life. I'm well aware that other pastors would have handled my arrogance in a very different way. If it hadn't been for his patience and wisdom, I'd probably be bitter and gone. When I was at my worst, he believed God was going to work in my life. He made a place for me to heal and grow. He saved my life.

The biggest change, though, has come in my relationship with God. He is, far more than ever, my life and breath. I sense His presence and His love, and I want to please Him in every thing I say and do. The lyrics of this song by Clint Brown perfectly describe the transition I've experienced in my walk with God:

The air that I breathe, my everything,

My hope, my soul, my all in all, O God.

My love, my life, my heart's desire,

My hope, my song, my all in all, O God.

I need you more in my life each day.

I need you more than my words can say.

If there's one thing I know for sure,

In my life I need you more.[2]

I tell Him every day that I want Him—not me—to be honored because He deserves all praise, honor, and glory. Instead of thinking God is lucky to have me on His side, I now wonder why He would stoop to use a moron like me.

Every day, I begin by opening my heart to the Lord and inviting Him to love me and lead me all day. When I go too long without sensing His presence, I can tell. For years, I didn't appreciate God's presence. In fact, I was so enamored with my ministry success and acclaim that I didn't even notice how much I missed Him. That's changed. The process of learning to be sensitive to His Spirit has been long and painful, but it has produced a wonderful intimacy with God. I often ask God to open my eyes to see His love and power. I ask Him for wisdom to do His will and the grace to get out of His way. I tell Him every day that I want Him—not me—to be honored because He deserves all praise, honor, and glory. Instead of thinking God is lucky to have me on His side, I now wonder why He would stoop to use a moron like me. (Paul said the same thing a little more eloquently when he called himself "the chief of sinners" God was using to reach the world with the gospel—1 Timothy 1:15-17.)

I hope you don't have to be put on God's operating table and cut open to have the tumor of self-sufficiency cut out of you, but my suspicion is that, sooner or later, virtually all of us come to this point in our lives. It happened to Abraham and to me, and it could happen to you. For a long time, I didn't listen to the people who loved me enough to tell me the truth. I wish I'd paid attention sooner, but I'm glad they were relentless in pursuing me. God pursued me through them.

I'd suggest you find a quiet place and ask yourself, "Am I pursuing God more passionately than anything else, including God's work?" I finally understood that God cared far more about my heart than all the work I wanted to do to build His kingdom. A second question is just as important: "Have I empowered people to speak into my life?" It's time to stop being defensive—either because we feel superior or we feel inferior. God has put some people in our lives to speak the truth to us . . . if we'll only listen. Being honest with God is sometimes exhilarating, but sometimes it's painful. Even if it's painful, take His message to heart. It's worth it.

Think about it...

1. What does it mean to be "broken and contrite"? Why does it take the work of God's Spirit for this to happen in our lives?

2. Have you experienced genuine brokenness? As you read this chapter, did you sense God was pointing out some area of your life that isn't fully surrendered to Him? If so, how would you describe the problem?

3. How would you answer these questions: Am I pursuing God more passionately than I'm pursuing anything else, including God's work? Have I empowered people to speak into my life?

4. Do you want a broken and contrite heart? Be honest. Talk to God about your answer.

Conclusion: What's Next?

As I've spoken to children's pastors and leaders on the topics in this book, they've had a range of responses. Some have said, "Let me at it!" They want to dive in and change things today. Others have responded, "The suggestions about strategy aren't as important as the issues of the heart. I really need to focus my attention on getting my heart right." And a few people have sadly said, "All this stuff is fine for other people, but I'm overwhelmed right now. I can't even think of adding anything else to my pile." Let me give some practical suggestions to each group.

The Eager

If you're ready to make all kinds of changes, slow down a bit. Pick one or two specific applications and focus on those until they become part of your life and ministry. Think, pray, and involve your team in the planning process. Then take steps to make the changes you and your team believe God wants you to make. After those are implemented and effective (after plenty of adjustments, I'm sure), you can pick two more goals and start the process with them. If you bite off too much at once, you'll confuse and demoralize your team. It's far better to build consensus and take slow steps of change.

The Convicted

The message of this book is much more about our hearts than strategies. If God has used my story to challenge you or inspire you, I'm thrilled!

Tell the Lord that you want to hear His voice and realize He often speaks through people who love you. When someone has the courage to tell you how much your behavior has hurt him, don't blow him off. Listen, ask for more input, and accept the painful reality that you've hurt those you love. When the full force of your sin and selfishness floods in, accept God's gracious forgiveness and trust Him to begin rebuilding your life. Don't confuse depression and brokenness. Depression is a sense of shame, helplessness, and hopelessness. Repentance begins with acknowledging painful realities, but a broken and contrite heart has the seed of hope that God forgives and restores. Temporary pain—even intense pain—can produce deep and lasting tenderness, peace, and wisdom. Let people in to correct you and then let them in to comfort and support you.

The Overwhelmed

I don't expect people to apply all the principles in this book in an afternoon. It's taken me twenty years, so give yourself some time and space! I talk to kids' pastors and leaders all the time who feel maxed out. They're incredibly busy, and they don't have an ounce of energy to do anything else. I suggest you take one point and apply it. In fact, the one I'd recommend is to focus on your relationship with God, enjoy His love for you in a fresh way, and let His grace overflow into the lives of others. Make sure first things are first, and your relationship with God is always first.

Are you ready? What's the next step for you? Go for it with all your heart, but be sure your first priority is to love God with everything in you. He deserves nothing less.

Endnotes

Chapter 1

1 Tim Keller, "The Man Who Would Not Be Hurried," a sermon delivered at Redeemer Presbyterian Church, December 17, 2000.

2 Larry Crabb, Finding God (Grand Rapids: Zondervan, 1993), 18.

Chapter 4

1 Rod Loy, First Assembly of God, North Little Rock, Arkansas.

2 George Barna, Transforming Children into Spiritual Champions (Ventura, California: Regal Books, 2003), 34.

3 John Tasch, "Training And Equipping Children," K! Magazine, Sept/Oct 2011.

Chapter 5

1 Charles H. Spurgeon, Spiritual Parenting (Whitaker House, 2003), cited on www.eaglecreekgroups.com/leaders.html, 11/11/11.

2 For much more on coordinating the family and the message of the church, see Reggie Joiner's material called Orange.

3 George Barna, "Parents Accept Responsibility for Their Child's Spiritual Development but Struggle with Effectiveness," www.Barna.org, May 6, 2003.

4 John Maxwell, Be a People Person (Colorado Springs: David C. Cook, 2007), 161.

Chapter 6

1 Many inventories are available online. For instance: www.churchgrowth.org.

2   For a copy of our church's Volunteer Application, contact me at www.briandollar.com.

3   For samples of job descriptions, contact me at www.briandollar.com.

Chapter 9

1   Denis Waitley, The Psychology of Winning (New York: Berkley Press, 1986), cited in The Lakeland Ledger, August 6, 1984, 16.

2   John Eldredge, Walking with God (Nashville: Thomas Nelson, 2010), 65.

Chapter 10

1   Frederick Wilcox, cited in The Legacy Leader by Anthony Lopez (First Book Library, 2003), 284.

2   John Ortberg, If You Want to Walk on Water You've Got to Get Out of the Boat (Grand Rapids: Zondervan, 2001), 162.

3   Andy Stanley, Next Generation Leader: 5 Essentials for Those Who Will Shape the Future (Colorado Springs: Multnomah Books, 2006), 63.

Chapter 12

1   A. W. Tozer, The Pursuit of God (Tribeca Books, 2011), 21.

2   Clint Brown, "The Air I Breathe," Live at Oak Tree, Daywind Records.

About the Author

Brian has been a Kids Pastor since 1992. His wife, Cherith, joined him in ministry in 1998. Together, they have passionately served kids and families in an effort to raise up a generation of life-long followers of Jesus Christ.

Brian approaches Kids Ministry with a cutting-edge style, leading a volunteer staff of over 150 in ministering to the children at First Assembly of God in North Little Rock, Arkansas. Every week, over 600 children gather for high-energy worship, games, and life-changing ministry from their dynamic ministry team.

In 1998, he founded High Voltage Kids Ministry Resources, which creates cutting-edge, multi-media, Children's Church curriculum, music, and videos. High Voltage Kids Ministry resources have been used in more than 5,000 churches across America.

Brian has a passion for training and equipping other Kids Ministry Leaders to be effective in their churches. He has been a featured speaker at many children's pastors' conferences, seminars, camps, and retreats.

Brian's Blog is found at www.briandollar.com. He uses the blog to coach other kids' ministry leaders by answering their questions weekly.

Brian and Cherith have been married for fourteen years. They have a daughter, Ashton, and a son, Jordan. They love spending time together, watching movies, and cheering for the Dallas Cowboys and Dallas Mavericks.

Resources for Kids Ministries

To Order More Copies

To order more copies of *I Blew It!*
go to www.influenceresources.com

For an opportunity to assess your children's ministry and find great
resources, visit MyHealthyChurch.com